WHY DOES THE OTHER LINE ALWAYS MOVE FASTER?

The Myths *and* Misery, Secrets *and* Psychology *of* Waiting *in* Line

WHY DOES THE OTHER LINE ALWAYS MOVE FASTER?

The Myths *and* Misery, Secrets *and*
Psychology *of* Waiting *in* Line

DAVID ANDREWS

WORKMAN PUBLISHING COMPANY
NEW YORK

Library of Congress Cataloging-in-Publication Data is available.

ISBN 978-0-7611-8122-4

Design by Becky Terhune
Jacket and interior images: Leontura/Getty Images

Workman books are available at special discounts when purchased in bulk for premiums and sales promotions as well as for fund-raising or educational use. Special editions or book excerpts can also be created to specification. For details, contact the Special Sales Director at the address below, or send an email to specialmarkets@workman.com.

Workman Publishing Co., Inc.
225 Varick Street
New York, NY 10014-4381
workman.com

WORKMAN is a registered trademark of Workman Publishing Co., Inc.

Printed in the United States of America

First printing October 2015

10 9 8 7 6 5 4 3 2 1

CONTENTS

CHAPTER ONE

The Taming of the Queue

A Life in Line

M any minds have explored the question of how we tame
the queue, which is to say: How do we reduce the
ubiquitous and obnoxious presence of line standing in our
lives? But I'm equally interested in a separate question:
How does the queue tame us?

The question first came to me circa summer 2002. I was
nineteen. My parents had driven up to visit me on Liberty
Weekend, the three days toward the end of boot camp at
Great Lakes Recruit Training Command (RTC), outside
of Chicago. This is when young sailors-in-training—
eager-beaver and hunting in packs in those sparkling
starched white uniforms they must all wear by decree—are
at last unleashed into the streets of suburban Chicagoland
for eight hours or so, before reporting back by five in the

evening, jazzed up for the first time in weeks on candy, matinee movies, Six Flags, and (for the lucky few) sex.

I wasn't much of a letter writer then, and all phone calls home I'd made were brief and perfunctory (not by choice; we had less than a five-minute window to use the pay phone once every two or three weeks), so my parents arrived with questions: So-o-o-o, how was boot camp? What was it like? What did we do in boot camp? Did I feel . . . different?

I stumbled. Boot camp was . . . but then didn't really know what to say that felt satisfying in any way. I'd learned the dead man's float. I knew the feel of pepper spray in my eyes and lungs from a macabre exercise they call the Confidence Chamber. I could now iron straight creases into shirts and fold clothes with a rigor and geometric exactitude mostly reserved for engineers and OCD sufferers. I'd learned some colorful new language, though little I could share with my parents. My shoes were so well

> The basic fact about human existence is not that it is a tragedy, but that it is a bore. It is not so much a war as an endless standing in line.
>
> —H. L. MENCKEN

polished, I could see my reflection in their tips. Beyond that, there wasn't much to report. I felt I had been through an exhausting ordeal, that I had somehow been changed, so it was a little mystifying to me that I had so little to say after seven-plus weeks.

"That's it? So what did they have you do all day?" my mother wanted to know.

"Um, well. A lot of standing. A lot of waiting. Standing in line. Standing in formation, which is like standing in line. It's not very interesting. It's actually extremely, extremely boring." This was true on all accounts.

"Waiting for what?"

"Waiting for the chow hall. For uniforms. For doctor exams, eye tests. For everything, really. A lot of the time they just make you wait until they tell you to stop waiting. Just stand in this line, and don't move until I command you to move."

"Ach. Lines." This was my father, his nostrils flaring with a note of disgust. A subject that always got his goat; the rant I'd heard countless times before: "Listen, I won't stand in them unless I absolutely have to. I've had enough lines for one lifetime. I'll come back later, rather than waste my time." My parents (and attendant children) had spent seven years living and working as expats in the post-Communist Romania of the 1990s, in which for various reasons (failures in market supply chains, a crippling bureaucracy left over from the days of Ceaușescu, et cetera) there were impossibly long lines for almost anything you can imagine: gas, eggs, milk, bread, the post office, currency exchange, visa renewal. Queuing was sort of the unofficial national pastime, placing third only to soccer and the American television import *Dallas* (both followed with a religious zeal: The streets emptied, businesses closed up shop, parents named sons J.R. and Bobby).

Having returned stateside, my father now abstains on principle. There is precious little in this life that's worth more than, say, five or ten minutes of his time. He's the sort who, under the guise of being helpful, will fill out customer service cards complaining of the delay—the businesses that have at some point filed away his criticisms must number in the triple digits by now.

"Well, you know, David," he said, in that manner that certain middle-aged fathers sometimes have: They have reasoned out the subject to its logical endpoint and will now impart to you in no uncertain terms the truth of the matter, which you will no doubt agree is just common sense. "The military is basically a socialist organization. The government—it pays you, feeds you, clothes you, provides your health care at no cost. No one's ever fired, no matter how incompetent. This is why there's so much waiting. No one's pressing them for quicker service. No one has to compete in the marketplace."

The lesson my father—a onetime business major, now a small-business owner moonlighting as the proud interim president of the Chamber of Commerce of an out-of-the way town on the West Coast with a population of 1,671—had arrived at from his time in Eastern Europe was that free markets liberated from government constraints cured a world of ills. In his mind, the word *citizen* is cousin to the word *customer*, and no businessman in his right mind would risk alienating his customer base with long lines. For him, the problem with "big government" is that it holds a monopoly and doesn't treat its citizens like customers. If only Washington were run like a business.

I didn't necessarily disagree with his assessment in this particular case, although I disagree with him on plenty of others. It was certainly true that I—lowly seaman recruit that I was—was no customer in the eyes of the military. No one was concerned with whether I was happy or not. In fact, keeping recruits unhappy is kind of the point.

But there was also certainly a lot more to this business of standing in line in the military than simply waiting for goods and services, something deeper. There had to be. In fact, the norms of how to stand in line are pretty much the first thing they teach you.

For example, here is what my first ten minutes of boot camp were like, after stepping off the shuttle that ferries new recruits from O'Hare International to RTC. The couple dozen of us newbies—dopey and doe-eyed, trying not to look terrified—were shepherded into the holding area of the Recruit In-Processing Center, a large, windowless, slate-gray hallway that reminded me of my rural Midwestern high school built in the architecturally utilitarian 1970s: austere, immediately forgettable, all possible distractions effaced to keep moony teenagers on task. All of us looked befuddled and shabby-looking, and not a few looked hungover (perhaps there'd been the inevitable last hurrah the night before, at the fleabag ashtray-smelling airport hotel contracted to service all incoming recruits), clutching duffel bags, wearing loose jeans and T-shirts with the names of rock bands or beer logos emblazoned on them.

Presently a tall first-class petty officer, a recruit division commander (the navy equivalent of a drill instructor), detached himself from a phalanx of other RDCs to direct traffic, barking in a loud, clipped, condescending voice (think R. Lee Ermey from *Full Metal Jacket;* the movie is nothing like my experience of boot camp, but I swear drill instructors model their bedside manner on him, as well as crib most of his best lines).

He directed us to stand in rows of three, backs to the wall. He was going to show us the three ways to wait: at attention, at parade rest, and at ease. For present purposes, at attention would be the most important—the one we should hold to until directed otherwise. Stand with your bodies erect, faces forward, legs straight, shoulders up and slightly back. Arms should be at your sides, hands in a balled fist with your thumbs just touching the outer seams of your pants legs. Heels should be touching and feet angled away from each other at 45 degrees. Keep forty inches between you and the person in front of you. Keep your eyes forward in a thousand-yard stare.

Other words of advice: Learn to use your peripheral vision. Never, but never, look a superior in the eyes, especially when in line. Speak only when spoken to, and never when standing at attention. Don't lock your knees (as I would learn one day when the person three bunks down from mine fell face-first onto the floor, giving himself a concussion). Always keep the bulkhead to your right. When two lines converge, "zipper in."

"Hurry up and wait," he told us, "is the unofficial motto of the United States armed forces." The tone of his voice said, *So get used to it*, capisce?

We didn't know this yet, but in ten minutes we'd learned the building blocks for our entire seven weeks of boot camp and arguably our entire military career. We would spend hours every day in this supremely uncomfortable position. At attention your feet hurt, your knees threaten to buckle, your lumbar region feels swollen to about the size of Wisconsin, and if anything itches, forget about it, because it's not going away, and you rarely know how long you have to stand like this, waiting, waiting, waiting. There is nothing to distract you from your boredom but the back of your shipmate's buzz-cut head. The tedium of it takes on an achy feverish presence.

My father later would say to me, "I bet if boot camp was run more like a business, you could all probably be in and out of there in two, three weeks, tops. None of that waiting around."

I myself would come to wonder, "So what the hell was the point of all that?" That's the question that led to this book.

TO QUEUE OR NOT TO QUEUE?

In line and on line. Formations, scrums, and mobs. The ways we wait. The ways we organize ourselves in space. What we choose to wait for and for how long. In the decade following my experience at boot camp, I would think often about lines, this odd business of queuing up. Does anyone else consider it a minor miracle that society doesn't break down into anarchy whenever a cashier opens an additional lane in a crowded supermarket?

Boot camp is simply one highly refined example of queueing. What I find more astonishing is simply how natural—how right—lining up seems to most of us in everyday civilian life. Few of us go through boot camp's rigorous reinforcement in the norms of how to wait, but we do it, and without much thought or fuss other than the usual cost/benefit analysis: Is this really worth the next fifteen minutes of my life? But as far as the structure of how we wait—usually in a line, back to front, with the first person to arrive served first—this goes mostly unquestioned.

The rightness of it seems self-evident. We learn this early and often, and we judge those who don't. One of the first times a child learns about injustice is when someone cuts ahead of her in the lunch line without consequence. In traffic we wish engine failure on those who wait until the last second to merge, on behalf of those of us already waiting patiently a mile before the bottleneck. But as anyone who has done much traveling abroad can attest, this propensity to form lines is far from universal to all cultures.

A few years ago, my wife and I flew to Amman, Jordan, to visit my wife's brother, then working there. One of those ancient Levantine cities where antiquity now meets (and sometimes butts heads with) the exigencies of modern finance and industry, Amman seemed to me at first jet-lagged glance a noisy bustling rumpus of a place—a hodgepodge of nationalities, cultures, religions, as well as an almost byzantine class structure, chockablock in a city that's struggling to contain them all. (In fact, the population of Amman is predicted to nearly triple in the next ten years, to 6.5 million—where will they put everyone?!)

The city is several thousand years old, from the age before centralized city planning (well, if you don't count the Romans, but what they've mostly left behind in Amman are ruins, rutted coliseums, and the rare standing colonnade you can pay about a buck to see and touch). There are no city grids, at least as we think of them. The streets and narrow alleys that trace twisting webs around Amman's nineteen hills teem with pedestrians and vehicles, for whom traffic laws, if any, are decidedly laissez-faire. A roadmap of Amman looks not unlike an ant farm, and on the street it often feels like you're in one. In older parts of the city, where streets are narrower, traffic slows to a slog of diesel fumes, honking, and general peevishness; my brother-in-law tells me that the dominant mood and driving mode there is "pissed-off caution." Everything and everyone—shops, street vendors, pedestrians, drivers—moves in claustrophobically close proximity to one another, under a parching ever-present sun that seems to hang about a foot over your head.

This is all to say that, though I came to be fond of the city by the end of my stay, those first few days there were extremely jarring and disorienting, and any crowded public interaction seemed to me a fight for my life and my sanity. Going to order lunch at a fast-food falafel joint, for instance, was a hectic experience. What was I doing wrong? Feeling jostled, I was attempting to squeeze my body down into the tightest possible space, sucking in my gut, with arms pulled in to my sides to limit exposure to the scrum of other people. The people were crowding me, invading my personal space. They were pushing past me as if I weren't there. In short, I was getting no closer to lunch.

Later I asked my brother-in-law about the situation. Does no one think of forming lines in Jordan? Surely that would make things a hell of a lot easier. Some pylons, some velvet rope. Instabarriers to direct traffic. Maybe one of those take-a-number dispensers? At the very least, it would be less taxing on the nerves. How did he handle it?

"Oh, you've just got to push your way," he said, after thinking about the question. "Budge and hustle your way to the front. I mean, there are lines in some places. Mostly rich people places. Class plays a crazy-huge role here. Businesses that cater to rich people have pretty well-defined lines and people wouldn't dare disrespect them. Places for the nonrich, though, can be insanely chaotic and it's seen as fairly OK to do a bit of elbowing and badgering to the front. But when I go to the bakery counter at an upscale supermarket, I don't really have to worry. I mean, there you don't really have a line either, not a physical line at least, but everyone knows the order of who came when, and will help the server know who to serve next. And we all get to feel a collective sense of smug bourgeois virtue for this."

There are also other considerations as to who gets served and in what order, he explained, ones that as an American he's still not fully keyed in on. For instance, if you know the clerk, or are related to him in some way, you're more likely to be waved ahead to the front of the counter, something my brother-in-law believes probably has to do with the importance of tribes and tribalism in Jordanian society. Elders also often get first dibs. Gender roles are very important in Jordan, so waiting areas with only women, or only men, or mixed company, will each have different codes of conduct—you'd never, ever see a woman elbowing her way to the front of a mixed-gender scrum.

"Oh, and if you have small children," he said, snapping his fingers as if he just thought of it, "Jordanians love children. Love, love, love them. If I ever have to do anything that involves the Jordanian government—get my visa renewed, for example—it can take me hours. But I have a British friend with a kid, a two-year-old, and he always brings his two-year-old along, and it takes him literally minutes. Zip. Right to the front of the line."

So much depends on context in Jordan, he said. Amman is so busy and overcrowded and changing at such a quick clip, it's difficult for an American to wrap his head around many of these things. He'd been there for nine months, and he still struggled most days. He would be tempted to call it chaos, but that's only because, as a foreigner, it's difficult to decipher the nuances of public interaction—in fact, in a lot of ways Jordanian culture is a lot more structured, or at least more complicatedly structured. In America, most businesses take only one thing into consideration: Who arrived first?

Who's to say what's better? Some expats, I imagine, rather like Amman's liveliness. By the end of my stay, I did too.

SOCIAL CUES

So why is it that some cultures or populations have such a highly developed and rigorous ethos of line standing (the Brits, say, who even alone, as a wit once quipped, "form a queue of one"), while others, like most Jordanians, have none? Surely there must be a story there—a history of line standing. Was there ever a time before lines in our culture, and if so, when and how did they become so deeply ingrained in our cultural psyche?

Much later, after both boot camp and Jordan were far behind me, I would be introduced in a graduate linguistics seminar to the field of nonverbal communications and would learn that, from an anthropological viewpoint, such seemingly banal and little-thought-about activities as line standing are indeed forms of communication. The way people organize themselves in space, even the look of their roads and cities (Amman's ant farm or America's boxy grids), telecasts the presiding values and beliefs of a society—how it conceptualizes and communicates issues of equality and fairness and personal independence, say, or even how its people understand and experience space and time.

It was anthropologist Edward T. Hall in the 1960s who first made the distinction between cultures that are low-context and monochronic, and cultures that are high-context and polychronic. The former comprise Americans, Brits, Germans, Scandinavians, and a small handful of others. The latter—the Jordanians and just about everyone else in the world. The two categories roughly correspond

Jumping the Queue In Britain

British social anthropologist Kate Fox, for her book *Watching the English*, took it upon herself to study the norms of British culture by personally and very systematically breaking Britain's holiest of unspoken social taboos. Without a doubt the most harrowing exercise for her—the one most antithetical to her existence, and by implication, to that of all British—was, what else? Cutting in line.

As she puts it: "Just the thought of queue-jumping was so horribly embarrassing that I very nearly abandoned the whole project rather than subject myself to such an ordeal. I just couldn't bring myself to do it. I hesitated and agonized and procrastinated, and then even when I thought I had managed to steel myself, I would lose my nerve at the last minute, and slink humbly to the back of the queue, hoping no one had noticed that I had even been considering jumping it."

If the news is to be believed, even the unruly, unsavory side of British society obeys this taboo—for instance, the recent London riots saw hoodie-wearing hooligans patiently waiting their turn to step through broken shop windows to filch electronics. Or else note the report from the BBC last year, when Scottish police were alerted to the fact that a broken ATM machine was spilling out banknotes, with people by the dozens queuing to receive the money.

to how a person perceives time and orients herself to the people around her. While the categories won't perfectly fit every individual in all situations—these are tendencies, not laws—they do explain why cultures broadly organize themselves in predictable ways that are fairly unique to that culture.

For instance, the fact that Americans generally stand in more or less orderly single-file lines reveals us to be largely monochronic low-context thinkers—we are wont to attend to one task at a time. As the word implies (*mono-* meaning single, *chronic* from the Greek word for time) we have a very static idea of time: We think of it as something that is fixed, rigid, a fact of nature the same for everyone, which ticks away whether we attend to it or not. We even perceive time as a queue—a straight timeline with important dates lined up in sequential order like so many orderly line standers.

A queue is a way of segmenting our activities according to a timetable: I will filter out everything but this single task, and when I am done with this task, I will move on to another one in due time. As low-context thinkers, we treat everyone, and expect to be treated ourselves, more or less equally and one at a time. The cashier's only consideration is "Who's next in line?" and ideally she'll treat each customer just like any other. We don't usually cater to the complex calculations that a Jordanian might make in a given social situation.

In contrast, polychronic high-context societies make allowances with regard to the context of the situation—who's waiting, what's their particular circumstance, what deference is owed to them due to their position in society? Societal traditions play a much larger role. As far as managing time is concerned—time for them is a loose construct, more fluid and subjective, based in interpersonal relationships and traditions. Whereas monochronic people are more likely to focus on one thing at a time and take time commitments seriously, polychronic people will juggle several things at once, take their personal commitments more seriously than their time commitments, ignore timetables, and wait in ways that appear disorderly to us.

They may seem similar, but polychronicity is not the same thing as the much vaunted multitasking. The difference is in our cultural conception of time. Do we serve time, as monochronicity demands (because time is fleeting), or does time serve us, as polychronicity demands? If anything, multitasking reveals a more slavish obedience to time constraints: One works on multiple things in order to make more efficient use of time (something polychronic societies are less likely to value). The multitasker, as the name suggests, remains task oriented, not people oriented.

Do You Stand *in* Line or *on* Line?

Our language often encodes our cultural norms as metaphor. For instance, when we stand *in* line, what are we in, exactly? Do we think of a line as a sort of walled-off space, with an inside and outside? If so, this might explain why the British call cutting in line "jumping the queue," which implies a barrier of some sort.

Or are we in line the same way we are *in* a relationship or *in* a motorcycle gang—part of a group governed by a certain social code?

In any case—and most likely the truth is a little of each—our unconscious attitudes toward lines affect how we visualize the space and people around us. It's interesting, then, that there are some regional American dialects—particularly in the Northeast—where people

Not only does this go a long way toward explaining why Jordanians lack a culture of line standing, but it might also answer that older question of mine: Why so much line standing in boot camp? Could it be that the reason is not, as my father would have it, because the military is a hoary old machine full of bureaucratic inefficiencies (though it is that, too, certainly) but because line standing serves to reprogram its recruits to think and do differently? To train recruits to be even more don't stand *in* line but rather *on* line, which changes the metaphor entirely. Instead of a sort of imaginary box or passageway you stand within, there's an imaginary line people stand on top of—so no inside and outside.

My pet theory? This variation perhaps points to a time when line standing was not as universal among English speakers as it is now. When simply following the orders of, say, one's drill sergeant, standing *on* a line makes perfect sense—it's an easy way for him to communicate how he wants you to stand. But once a culture begins to be more fully habituated to the concept of line standing—when it begins to feel natural—then it begins to conceive of a line as a walled-off space, with rules that govern the behavior of people within that space.

monochronic and low-context, in other words. But why would they want that?

According to the *Marine Corps Drill and Ceremonies Manual* (which the Navy has shared since 1974), the main purpose of drill—which I am tempted to call queuing by another name: they are two species of the same genus, born of the same genetic ancestor—is to promote discipline, good order, and group cohesion. It also, I would add, teaches patience, an important virtue in all areas of military life. But perhaps most important, lines are simply a pragmatic means of managing the thousands of recruits who go through this rite annually, a form of crowd control built into the DNA of military culture.

Think of a muddle-minded nineteen-year-old—or better yet, think of fifty thousand of them—thrown into this vast machine whose organizational complexity can confound the best and brightest minds. A machine, moreover, that must make sure that all these nineteen-year-olds are clothed and fed and trained properly, and according to schedule. How are all these muddle-minded hormonally charged nineteen-year-olds supposed to make heads or tails of any of this? They can't see the big picture, visualize the entire operation in its totality. Well, yeah, who can? To do so would be nearly paralyzing. From the seaman recruit to the drill instructor to the four-star admiral—the machine is designed so that each employee needs to understand little more than military basics and the job required of him (though obviously the job scales up in scope with each pay grade).

In short, queueing is a way of ensuring that a nineteen-year-old recruit is never lost. Once he learns the basics, after the first week or so, he is never put in a situation where he doesn't know how to conduct himself. Wait here, do this, and when you're done in this line, go wait in that other one.

Boot camp isn't nearly as difficult as it's portrayed in the movies. Just one thing at a time, one foot in front of the other. Any idiot who can tie his own shoelaces will make it through just fine. The military is probably one of the most monochronic and low-context organizations you can think of (outside of an assembly line, perhaps), and boot camp generally runs like clockwork for it. As one of my RDCs would tell us almost hourly, "This ain't rocket science." Borrowing from the name given to the brainy eggheads bound for a career as nuclear engineers on submarines—recruits with a reputation for overintellectualizing any given task—we were constantly told, "Don't 'nuke' it."

The days of individual feats of heroism in battle died sometime around the late Renaissance, as fiefdoms gave way to nation-states, and knights to conscripted armies. As the Romans had discovered a long time before, the more reliable fighting force is the one with large numbers and a highly developed system of order and discipline. The ability to follow a rigid schedule became more important than horse riding. How a soldier stood among others became more important than how well he wielded a sword. It's also probably better that the average soldier doesn't understand the *why* of it, which might lead to second-guessing. The *what* is more than enough, and the simpler the better.

Over time, armies began to break things down into their simplest components: Who's next in line?

There's a lot to be said for military order and line standing has a lot to say for it. For one thing, it's usually egalitarian. In boot camp, everyone is treated like shit, but they're treated like shit equally according to rank, and you rarely have to worry that someone is getting more than his fair share. You don't have to do much "networking" to get ahead in your work life (though sucking up will help on occasion). You do this incredibly simple task right, and you're guaranteed a paycheck, with the possibility of moving further up the ranks. As a dumb nineteen-year-old college dropout who could barely feed or dress himself, for whom the future was a paralyzing maze of choices, I found the simplicity of military life a relief. I rarely had to worry about what I was supposed to be doing next. It was a way of putting off the messiness of civilian life for a while.

But this line of thinking leads to the darker side of military life as well: The first step of training is to quash the recruit's sense of individuality, because individualism leads to disorder. Everyone must look the same, be the same. The implied imperative: Obey; don't question. In the form of a line, recruits are being trained to be the cogs in a machine, deprogrammed away from that humanistic ideal we were taught in kindergarten: "Everyone is special." Not

To Queue or Not to Queue

My own disquiet about the alienating effect of standing in line may be a reflection of my nationality, and the words we use: "stand in line." At least that's the conclusion of Robert J. C. Young—a British academic who emigrated to the U.S.—when reflecting on the difference between the word *queue* and its American equivalent. He believes the difference colors our perception of line standing. He takes special note of the fact that *queue* can be both noun and verb, and it doesn't require a preposition: Brits can say either "the man stood in a queue" or simply "the man queued." Americans could say, "the man stood in a line," but it would sound strange to say, "the man line-stood."

A small difference, perhaps, but Young thinks it's big enough. To "stand in line" implies "that this is something you have to submit yourself to, that you lose in some sense your own power to act as an individual or even as a group at some point." But by saying "the man queued," you imply that the man chose to queue, or at least agreed to queue. He is not powerless in that construction. "If you queue," Young writes, "you remain linguistically and in some broader, important sense an agent, an active subject, part of a particular social consensus about how to behave in a particular situation that requires some measure of equality and fairness to all."

Young argues that maybe we shouldn't think of queueing and standing in line as synonyms at all. Standing in line bespeaks rigid adherence to rules, navy recruits all in a row. Queueing is softer, a spontaneous act of common agreement that allows for exceptions to the rule of first come, first served. Young recollects the line he stood in at the airport immigration office—in which most of the line standers were British—when he was moving to New York. A harried-looking Englishman asked permission to jump the line because his daughter was getting married in an hour. He asked this of each person in line as he moved to the front. Amazingly, no one objected, and the father of the bride moved up to the front in less than a minute. In that moment, Young writes, "the line had been turned into a queue."

"Americans love to laugh at the British and their queues," he concludes, "but that is because when they see them queueing, they only see them standing in line."

anymore, you ain't. Ask anyone at the DMV or in the security line at the airport: Isn't there something dehumanizing about line standing? It purports to treat everyone equally, but in the way that cattle are treated equally. The world described in Orwell's *1984* is similar to the one a recruit enters: a world of line standing, of a bureaucracy without end, of pragmatic crowd management, of soul-crushing monotony, of mindless conformity.

It's a comfort, sure, but at what cost to your humanity?

An old army joke, one that dates back to at least the 1960s: The sergeant was preparing the discharge papers

> I like the idea that people in New York now have to wait in line for movies. You go by so many theaters where there are long, long lines. But nobody looks unhappy about it. It costs so much money just to live now, and if you're on a date, you can spend your whole date time in line, and that way it saves you money because you don't have to think of other things to do while you're waiting and you get to know your person, and you suffer a little together, and then you're entertained for two hours. So you've gotten very close, you've shared a complete experience. And the idea of waiting for something makes it more exciting anyway. Never getting in is the most exciting, but after that waiting to get in is the most exciting.
>
> —ANDY WARHOL,
> *THE PHILOSOPHY OF ANDY WARHOL*

for a batch of draftees whose term of service was up. "I'll bet you guys are just waiting for these papers to go through so you can punch me in the nose," he said. "Not at all, sergeant," replied one of the men. "I promised myself that once I got out of the army I'd never stand in line again."

After the military, I, too, promised myself I'd never stand in line again. (Good luck fulfilling that promise!) I returned to college, let my hair grow out, and otherwise resolutely left the military behind me. I studied literature and philosophy, in part because both of those subjects seemed as diametrically opposite the military lifestyle as possible.

The strange thing? Despite my efforts to avoid it, the subject of standing in line, of waiting and boredom without end, kept creeping up in the literature I was studying, however obliquely or tangentially. At least they seemed to capture what I felt when I was in the military.

In the twentieth century, philosophers wrote treatises on the experience and emptiness of time. Novelists the world over took up the subject of waiting, going inward into the contents of characters' minds, as opposed to what happens to their bodies, probably spurred by the realization that, on any given day at any given hour, nothing much happens! Time ticks away; minutes and hours pass; thoughts are thought, feelings felt. This is what happens when we wait. This, truly, is the condition of modern life. It is to many of these writers' credit that they so often make these supposedly empty moments seem thrilling.

When I tell people about my weird obsession with lines, there is almost always an initial moment of confusion. Huh? Say again?

"Standing in line?" I struggle to explain. "Queueing? Waiting for things? You know, that thing you do in one form or another almost every single day of your life?" What? Really? Why would I be interested in that? But then, after I've better described what I mean—surprise—everyone inevitably seems to have a wealth of anecdotes, trivial daily annoyances, observations to share. Obviously, there is more to their experience of line-standing than they think.

Lines are the wallpaper of daily life, the music you tune out in the grocery store. They are everywhere, yet they work best when they're invisible, innocuous, unobtrusive. (And when they're not? We want heads on pikes, bums booted out of office.) But queues in one shape or another are essential to the machinery of modern life. As I found after leaving the military, like it or not, there is no escape.

So let us now insert this background feature—the queue—into the foreground. What are we really doing when we queue?

Kafka, Patron Saint of the Queue—and of This Book

Without a doubt, a patron saint of the queue—and hence of this book—would have to be Franz Kafka, whose central characters fall victim to unseeable bureaucratic machinations, waiting, waiting, waiting, for decisions that are out of their hands, by decision makers whom they never meet, for reasons that are utterly opaque. I first encountered Kafka's writing soon after separating from the navy. It was a revelation. Though Kafka never wrote about the military, exactly, it seemed he was rendering perfectly the absurd and sometimes crazy-making experience of being processed by the military bureaucracy. It's little wonder that Kafka would become so important in the twentieth century and the so-called age of machines. After all, the military isn't the only institution with an outsize bureaucracy.

Take his novel *The Castle,* for instance. Through a bureaucratic mix-up, a land surveyor known only by the name of K. is called to a village ruled by a nearby castle. The castle works according to a bizarre bureaucracy full of absurd and arcane rules that K. is unable to make heads or tails of, because no one understands it in its totality. The villagers simply follow its orders with an almost religious faith that the castle—and the decisions it makes—are flawless (even when that position is patently absurd). Only K. pushes back against this belief by seeking an audience with the castle bureaucrats to explain his predicament.

The entire novel is the story of K. trying—and abjectly failing—to get an answer, scurrying through hamster wheels within hamster wheels of nightmarish bureaucratic procedure, waiting for administrators who never show their faces. A novel made up entirely of waiting, in other words. Like most of Kafka's work, there is no resolution; by the end of the novel, the reader is left with waiting without end, never even having seen the promised land. Depending on the reader, the novel can be exhausting, horrifying, or hilarious (sometimes all three at once).

Kafka would have been well acquainted with the effect of living in a bureaucracy. After all, he was a clerk under the Kingdom of Bohemia, where he filed insurance claims for the Worker's Accident Insurance Institute, day in and day out. In other words, he was part of the labyrinthine workings of the modern bureaucratic state at the front end of the twentieth century. No wonder his work became so influential. Today, we regularly call bureaucratic nightmares Kafkaesque, as if he were personally responsible for the Department of Motor Vehicles.

CHAPTER TWO

THE BIRTH OF THE QUEUE
Bread Lines, Assembly Lines, Lunch Lines

Noah may have led the animals in the queuelike "two and two of all flesh" onto the ark, but there was no precise word for this (at least in English) until the modern era.

In 1755, when Samuel Johnson compiled his meticulous, nigh-exhaustive dictionary of the English language (the first of its kind, too modestly titled: *A Dictionary of the English Language* should've been *The Dictionary of the English Language*), he listed around two dozen definitions of the word *line*. Some of these definitions remain familiar to us ("longitudinal extension," "marks in the hand or face," "the string that sustains the angler's hook," a line of text), and some not ("one tenth of an inch," "lint or flax"). But nowhere does the word *line* refer to the act of people standing sequentially in wait. As for the word *queue*—more

appropriate, given that Dr. Johnson was an Englishman—
he gives no entry for it.

The modern concept of the queue probably first made
entry onto English shores circa 1837, transported from
France via the pen of the great Victorian polymath Thomas
Carlyle. He was writing his odd, expansive history of the
French Revolution, the events of which had happened
roughly four decades prior. And what does Carlyle focus
his attention on? Sure, sure, guillotines sent heads rolling;
mobs seemed to rise up willy-nilly in the streets; Jacobins
in general made a muck of things. Of course.

But another thing also catches his eye: "If we look now
at Paris, one thing is too evident: that the Bakers' shops
have got their Queues, or Tails; their long strings of pur-
chasers, arranged in tail, so that the first come be the first
served." The modern reader might scratch his head at this
description. Would Carlyle's British audience have been
unaware of the concept of standing in line? Apparently.

A revolutionary idea for a revolutionary time. Carlyle
seems pretty taken by the notion. "In time," he writes, "we
shall see it perfected by practice to the rank almost of an
art; and the art, or quasi-art, of standing in tail become one
of the characteristics of the Parisian People, distinguishing
them from all other Peoples whatsoever." Elsewhere he
admires the French mob for being so "rapid, audacious;

Waiting in Tail

The word *queue* comes from the Latin *cauda,* meaning tail. The British wouldn't have been entirely ignorant of the word before Carlyle, even if it wasn't in Samuel Johnson's dictionary. In the eighteenth century, the queue was a fairly common hairstyle, one that was mandatory for all British soldiers and sailors. They would pull their hair back into extremely long and extremely tightly braided pigtails and then dip these tails in tar or candle wax to keep them straight.

Few were sad to see the hairdo die. The military first reduced the length of the tail to seven inches and then a few years later ordered their removal entirely. This reprieve from the queue was greeted with joy and jubilation. One former soldier recalls the braids being so uncomfortably tight, his first time in the chair the barber told him, "Keep your eyes shut, you young blackguard, till I have finished, or you will not be able to close them after." As someone else wryly noted, the queue was "a preposterous and most unwarlike method of dressing hair."

so clear-sighted, inventive, prompt to seize the moment; instinct with life to its finger-ends! That talent, were there no other, of spontaneously standing in queue, distinguishes, as we said, the French People from all Peoples, ancient and modern." Huh?

I wonder whether Carlyle is half joking in his hyperbole. Consider the times. The lines Carlyle describes are "Baker's-queues": the lines people formed waiting for bread. If "standing in tail" was an art, it sure wasn't an elective one.

Widespread famine and massively destabilizing social changes were sending the new revolutionary government into a tailspin. The first industrial revolution in France decades before had brought thousands upon thousands into the city in a great broiling urban mass. Bread was hugely important, as it was the average peasant's main form of sustenance, on which he spent most of his meager income. Bread riots were not infrequent when grain crops failed and prices rose. Often the bread was of poor quality, as bakers mixed in sawdust, dirt, even sometimes manure to make up for the lack of flour. Sometimes there would be no bread at all for weeks at a time, and then what were people supposed to do? They were hungry. These "Baker's-queues" represented widespread failures. (Whose failures, though? This remained the question of the day.)

Carlyle asks the reader to consider the plight of the peasant, who not only struggles to make the most subsistence-level living, but then must "stand waiting (if his wife is too weak to wait and struggle) for half-days in the Tail, till he get it changed for dear bad bread!" It should come as no surprise, then, that "controversies, to the length sometimes of blood and battery, must arise in these exasperated Queues."

But to stand in queue was not simply an act of hungry necessity. This was also a political act, ideologically charged with meaning. Nearly every political protest movement finds novel ways of organizing people in space. In our own age, we've had sit-ins and walkouts, the clockwise circles that striking union workers make in front of factory gates, and the many marches on Washington. These actions are invested with meaning. At the very least, they communicate solidarity. The slogan of the French Revolution was "Liberty, Equality, Fraternity": To patiently wait one's turn was to hold everyone as equals. (In America, we believe that all are created equal. So too—perhaps—do we stand in line.)

"Patriotism stands in queue," wrote Carlyle. He was channeling the revolutionary propaganda that was being circulated at the time. In response to conspiracy theories about the cause of grain shortfall—caused, some then argued, by "secret Royalists" still loyal to the deposed king—the official answer is to form more "Baker's Queues, by and by, more sharp-tempered than ever."

In a complex metaphor, the "tail" is conceived of as a literal rope that everyone holds onto for dear life. But outside forces ("mischievous, deceitful persons," i.e., secret

Royalists) will seek to cut the rope, so that the queue becomes unraveled. So the rope must be instead made "of iron chain." To borrow an idiom from another context (namely, American football), the French mob is literally being asked to "hold the line." The queue, then, becomes a metaphor for this new fledgling egalitarian society. Hold fast, or the straight line will unravel into a mob (and not the good kind that Carlyle admires).

Still, however high-minded this act of solidarity was, Carlyle can't help but note that the poor seemed to bear the brunt of most of the waiting. Elsewhere, the rich continued to eat as well as ever, "heated with excess of high living," and the Jacobins were busy throwing parades as the government collapsed around them. Might not these poor noble line standers do better for themselves, he suggests, marching their queues straightaway to the mansions of these oh so rich and mighty?

LA NAISSANCE DE LA QUEUE

I wonder: Would Carlyle have written so rapturously about the queue if he had not written his book in London? At the time, it was the biggest and busiest city the world had ever known.

Elsewhere, in a letter to his wife, he characterized London as "that Devil's oven with its dirts and noises. The disgusting dearth of London, the noise, unwholesomeness, dirt, and fret of one's whole existence there has often forced itself upon me." Famously, he had a soundproof room constructed in the attic of his London residence to escape from the noise of the street, so that he could write in relative peace. However wonderful a writer he could be, Carlyle had a reputation for being somewhat of a crank. As such, perhaps he saw in the queue a possible respite from the hell that is other people.

So what would have been the state of line standing in London or the United States? What we know is that Carlyle certainly found the queue noteworthy, as did others. That itself is noteworthy. As late as 1854, an American visitor to France, in a book about his journeys, wrote about the curiosity of standing *en queue* (the italics are his, emphasizing the concept's foreignness) with a group of college students at the entrance of a library, enforced by a barrier that lets through only one person at a time. How was it? He reported feeling "half impatience," an "uneasiness of the body," and "an occasional pleasant jeu d'esprit," the sense of camaraderie that results when witty young people share a boring experience with one another. Sounds about right.

"Verily 'they manage such things better in France,'" complained a flustered correspondent to the London architectural magazine *The Builder* in 1851, bemoaning the state of crowd control in England. "Pray lift up the voice of your powerful journal," he implored, "against disgraceful carelessness of arrangement which causes such perilous crushing at the doors of our public places of resort." He had recently been to a public event at Windsor, where "it was quite humiliating to hear the Frenchmen and their ladies, when crushed and bruised, and tossed to and fro, remark bitterly upon the stupidity of a nation which calls itself great." He advocated the French model of "la queue."

So are the French responsible for the birth of the queue? How convenient it would be to assign blame. It does seem that the queue remained quintessentially French for much of the early nineteenth century, local color for the guidebooks. We can't say exactly when queueing caught on in places like England or the United States, but it was almost certainly in the latter half of the nineteenth century. History can be maddeningly (if unsurprisingly) opaque on these more banal everyday sorts of things.

Still, I find the fact that one of the first (if not the first) descriptions of the act of line standing in English happened in the context of the French Revolution just about perfect. After all, the revolution is frequently cited as the maelstrom that inaugurated the modern era. In its wake, nations formed, monarchies were deposed, democracy spread far and wide. Around the globe, how people lived—and, maybe more important, how they worked—changed dramatically in the hundred years preceding and following the revolution. The lines we wait in are the by-product of this modern life and also one of its most emblematic symbols.

The queue went over like gangbusters. But why? What are the conditions of modern life, particularly in the nineteenth century, that gave rise to the queue? Let's explore some options, each of which adds only a part of the story of why and how we wait today.

A RESPONSE TO COGNITIVE OVERLOAD

Beginning in the eighteenth century, great mills and factories transformed skylines, and cities around the globe metastasized massively around them, becoming the modern metropolises we know them as today (Paris, London, New York City, Tokyo, Milan . . .).

Amid the buzz of industrial innovations and technological marvels (the lightbulb! the daguerreotype! the phonograph! flushable toilets!), a thoroughly modern problem presented itself: What do we do with all these freakin' people? Huge influxes of new residents from all over moved into the cities, millions of them in a big broiling mass, the great majority of them the working poor.

Never before had so many people lived in such close proximity to one another.

The infrastructure of these cities (especially London, which annoyed Carlyle so much) wasn't sufficient to hold everyone. As a result, places like London were overcrowded, undergoverned, dirty, dangerous, noisy, and wild, wild, wild. Charles Dickens—that prodigious walker of London streets—may have written of his fellow boisterous Londoners that they "revel in a crowd of any kind," but the experience was clearly not to everyone's tastes.

Joseph Amato, in his history of walking, characterizes the urban street of the nineteenth century as "a dangerous landscape of swiftly altering situations, amid a kaleidoscope of sounds, sights, shifting currents of people, and moving objects." The city street was an all-purpose sort of environment: an avenue for traveling, a place of work and entertainment, a marketplace, the space where neighbors gathered to gossip.

This was where street vendors, smiths, prostitutes, pickpockets, beggars, street entertainers, and the like fed off the energy of the ever present crowd, which swelled around them in alternating currents, an impressive force that, according to Dickens, "swings you to and fro, and in and out, and every way but the right one." Seen from afar, these crowds were magnetic, majestic, and not infrequently dangerous; they seemed to exhibit a character, a mood, independent of any single individual in the crowd.

The crowd could truly be impressive, but also a headache. Think cities have it bad now? In the beginning there were no traffic laws, zoning laws, noise ordinances; no sidewalks or crosswalks; no elevators, escalators, turnstiles, revolving doors, or any of the other ways that movement and commerce are regulated and coerced in the cities.

There was nothing separating people from traffic, meaning death by horse and carriage wasn't uncommon. There was no pressure to move in a straight line, by city design, by force of law, or by force of custom. Someone might bob and weave, make a beeline toward a street vendor, then turn sharply right when he sees someone he knows on the other side of the street. Each of these small movements, actions, gestures have a ripple effect on the crowd, which must alter its movement accordingly. The urban walker as a result, says Amato, had to "master the art of ducking and dodging." Sound exhausting? It was.

In short, to live in a city like London or New York was to experience an "overload on cognitive capacities." This is the phrase used by the social psychologist Stanley Milgram in his study "The Experience of Living in Cities" (written in the relatively placid year of 1970). Simply put, the city provides too much for the senses to take in all at once, too many people. Milgram's argument was that an urban population eventually adopts cultural and psychological survival mechanisms to deal with it all, mechanisms that sharply distinguish the behavior of someone living in a city from someone living in the country or a small town. His theory explains, for instance, why New Yorkers have a reputation for being brusque.

So what are those mechanisms? The first Milgram notes is the tendency of city dwellers to "deal with one another in highly segmented, functional terms, and of urban sales personnel to devote limited time and attention to their customers." When living in a city, you simply have more people to contend with; you don't have time or the mental resources to chat with some stranger about the weather or to suffer scrums lightly. You tend to deal with people one at a time, and in terms of the task at hand. Next customer!

The second survival mechanism is the "acceptance of noninvolvement, impersonality, and aloofness in urban life." Elsewhere Milgram calls this condition anonymity. In a city, who has the time to get to know everyone? You don't want to have to tip your hat to everyone you pass, or make idle chitchat with someone you don't know for the three minutes you two mutually wait for your lattes at Starbucks. You don't have the emotional energy to actually care about (or judge, for that matter) what another stranger is up to, so why bother? Adopt the thousand-yard stare. Immerse yourself in your iPhone. The queue as practiced in places like New York City (face-to-back, proper distance established, eye contact avoided) helps establish and reinforce these conditions of anonymity.

The third survival mechanism relates to changes in the city dweller's cognitive processes. Examples include "his inability to identify most of the people he sees daily, his screening of sensory stimuli . . . and his selectivity in responding to human demands." The city very literally changes how one thinks and acts, and a large part of that change is filtering out the things that don't pertain to your task. The line allows you to become single-minded. You don't want to have to be constantly negotiating with the scrum to get what you need.

The last survival mechanism is competition. Because of limited resources and facilities, life in the city is determined by "the subway rush; the fight for taxis; traffic jams; standing in line to await service" and other assorted headaches. Why should I let you in when I was here first? People in cities become more aggressive when someone tries to get more than their share, because everyone is in competition with everyone else, and a queue is one way of policing other's behaviors (partly through voluntarily subjecting yourself to them).

From personal experience, the concept of overload, and human adaptation to it, certainly rings true. When visiting New York City, for instance, there's always some point when I feel the need to return to my hotel room and submerge myself beneath a mile of pillows.

However, I think Milgram gets only part of the story. By attributing these mechanisms solely to psychology's role in shaping culture, he makes the queue seem all but foreordained, a natural response to a man-made environment. If so, why are there busy cities in other parts of the world where these features are notably absent? But I'm also curious about how city dwellers have been trained or conditioned to adopt these mechanisms, whether by laws, by custom, or by response to the city environment as it has been designed. Can both be true?

A RESPONSE TO WORK

The same economic forces that brought about our major metropolises also changed the nature of work for millions upon millions of people. The industrial revolution happened, in other words. The vast majority of people shifted from agriculture-based work to factory-based work, and it's nearly impossible to understate what effect this had on the cultural life of entire nations. This was the reason Edward Hall gave for why certain cultures became monochronic and low-context: places like England and Germany merely felt the effects of industrial change more acutely than others. How so?

For one thing, a worker's relation to time changes when you put him in the factory. Peasants go from task to task, and time might be measured according to those tasks (the time it takes to milk the cows, to bale the hay) in a way that isn't linear. There is no need to constantly check the clock.

But when you work in a factory, the thing that you are selling is your time: You agree to work for an employer x amount of hours for y amount of pay. The clock becomes the final arbiter around which you organize your day, not simply the accomplishment of certain tasks. (Computer Solitaire was invented for precisely this reason. How often have you found yourself waiting for the clock to wind down because there were no tasks left to accomplish?)

Plus, factories are often complex machines, necessitating that all the pieces are in place for them to function properly. Employers began to strictly enforce starting times, firing or reprimanding workers who were tardy; this necessitates better clocks and pocket watches (which the Swiss were happy to supply, from factories of their own), and the assurance that they are set to the same time, not always an easy proposition before the establishment of time zones. Time becomes measurable, and thus linear, monochronic.

Hence you also have a situation in which a mass of workers must all arrive at work at roughly the same time and leave at roughly the same time, creating a vast horde moving through the city roughly at the same time. Today's rush hour vehicular traffic was preceded by yesterday's rush hour foot traffic. The crush at the doors of buses. The traffic that clogs up the street. The workers crowd the gates of the factory before settling into a line to have their time cards punched. The workday has ramifications for the rest of the day. The worker is forced to do his banking during his lunch hour, and his grocery shopping after work, where he has to wait in line behind a dozen others doing the same. Lines, lines, and more lines.

And then there's the assembly line, dating back to the late eighteenth century (the automatic flour mills of Delaware, and the Portsmouth Block Mills and the Bridgewater Foundry in England . . .). As work became more mechanical, we did too. These factories divided labor into specialties, so that each worker focuses on a single solitary task, just one more spinning wheel in the machine. While the agrarian farmer (aided by his family) might have been responsible for almost all areas of farming the land, including the selling of his produce, in a modern production system, work in general becomes more specialized and segmented.

As corporations (and governments or any large organization, for that matter) expand, they need more than just workers to work the line. They need sales departments, accounting specialists, human resources, development, advertising, a secretarial labor pool. A modern economy would not function without these complex bureaucracies and supply chains, but they also increase the risk that you will be waiting for someone else to get anything accomplished, and that wait might very well take the form of a waiting room, or a line at the service desk, or the infuriatingly bland music you hear while your call is put on hold for the umpteenth time.

The final stick in the gut? The modern worker is paid for his time with money, which is not the case in a barter society. The factory worker may not have a lot of money (he almost certainly does not in the nineteenth century), but he probably has more of it than time (you know, with the twelve-to-fourteen hour workdays and all). Who, any longer, has time to grow the food he eats, to sew the clothes he wears? Instead, the worker has to haul his ass over to the store, where he buys food and clothing made in other factories, made by workers in a machinelike system similar to his own. And so, in the nineteenth century, we begin to see the first shopping culture, with the building of major department stores (Harrods in London, Marshall Field's in Chicago, Le Bon Marché in Paris . . .).

In short, the worker becomes also a consumer. And because there are several million other consumers in a given city, chances are he will find himself waiting at the store, too. Truly there is no escape.

MASS PRIVATION

Nobody stands in line for the fun of it, obviously. Lines are an unpleasantness borne out of necessity in the competition for limited resources. This is Economics 101, really. The breadlines in Paris were the result of a dire mismatch between supply and demand. People gotta eat. What's interesting is how so many of the countries that subsequently adopted an ethos of rigorous queueing (England and Russia are two examples that spring to mind) went through similar periods of prolonged hardship.

In *Ten Days That Shook the World*, John Reed's famous firsthand account of the Russian October Revolution in 1917, he reports that queueing there had been introduced during the reign of Czar Nicholas in 1915. However, he says, it was applied intermittently, in fits and starts. It really wasn't until 1917—the year of the revolution and of crippling shortages of food—that the queue "settled down as the regular order of things." Reed implores his American readership to "think of the poorly-clad people standing on the iron-white streets of Petrograd whole days in the Russian winter! I have listened in the bread-lines, hearing the bitter acrid note of discontent which from time to time burst up through the miraculous good nature of the Russian crowd . . ." He could be channeling Thomas Carlyle.

Meanwhile, what about the longstanding reputation the British have for being willing, patient—even eager practitioners of the art of line standing? A relatively recent fiction, it turns out. According to Joe Moran, author of the book *Queueing for Beginners*, this myth was propaganda propagated during World War II, a time of shortages and severe rationing. Queues were in fact often tense and politically charged affairs that had to be policed in case of riots. Fights broke out; people complained bitterly. Only after the war—flush with the triumph of winning "the good fight"—did people begin to view the queue more favorably, seeing in it a visual symbol of the "British tradition of decency, fair play, and democracy." It led the British to pat themselves on the back for taking the war like champs (when really, they whinged as much as any of us would).

But, as I mentioned, even when we're not in a time of

drought or war, scarcity is a fact of life in the city. Not scarcity of food, but scarcity of time, space, lanes of traffic, seats on the bus. Arguably, it is the repetitiveness of an action, over a prolonged period of time, by a significant proportion of the population, through which a temporary practice is established as the cultural norm.

A few years ago, the satirical news site The Onion published an article with the title "Nation Instinctively Forms Breadline." It was written in the wake of the financial recession; in the story, millions of people find themselves pulled by "a strange force they could neither resist nor describe" to form a two-thousand-mile-long line spanning seven states.

The article is funny, I think, because the scenario it describes seems almost (but never quite) plausible. We've seen the photographs: the breadlines, the employment office lines. Those lines are a constituent part of the story we tell about ourselves as a nation, and we feel this story (and the danger it represents) deeply. The Great Depression is only the most iconic example of hardship and scarcity. Really, our entire national history is underwritten by the cyclical regularity of our economic booms and then, tragically, busts. Might not these lean times have imprinted themselves on us as a culture?

DELIBERATE CITY DESIGN

At some point—dates vary from city to city and nation to nation—leaders within multiple countries decided that they had had enough of the irrational, sometimes violent rabble of their cities. But rather than simply saying, "Off with their heads!" (or whatever they might have said in the olden days), they began implementing slyer, more subtle ways of controlling human behavior and movement. In other words, they sought to deliberately tame the crowd. If the city dweller was going to behave like an animal, they would rather that animal be of a species that was docile, compliant, bovine. . . .

Often the reasons were not just pragmatic or cosmetic. Many reasonably surmised the revolutionary potential of the crowd. After all, popular uprisings were not limited to Paris, nor to 1789. Rome, Venice, Milan, Vienna, Budapest, Prague, Berlin, New York City (to name only a handful) all had their own recurring histories of mobs, melees, and massacres in the hundred or so years spanning both sides of the French Revolution. Seems that if you cram a million or so people who have many good reasons to be unhappy into a tight space together, things can get messy.

Linearity began to be imposed on the way people moved about in cities everywhere. Entire knots of neighborhoods, the small cramped winding medieval alleyways,

On Morality and the Straightness of Lines

If I mend at this rate, it is not impossible . . . but I may arrive hereafter at the excellency of going on even thus:

---

which is a line drawn as straight as I could draw it by a writing-master's ruler. . . .

This right line—*the path-way for Christians to walk in! say divines—*

—The emblem of moral rectitude! says Cicero—

—The best line! *say cabbage planters—is the shortest line, says Archimedes, which can be drawn from one given point to another.—*

So says Tristram Shandy, the eponymous narrator of Lawrence Sterne's strange and very funny novel from 1767. Shandy is lamenting his inability to tell the story of his own life straight. He keeps getting caught up in digression after digression, so that by the end of his quite lengthy autobiography, he has barely gotten past the moment of his birth. As his quote suggests, his own inability to proceed in a straight line is a failure of morality and reason (not to mention pragmatic storytelling)

As English speakers (I can't speak for other languages), we perhaps have the tendency to conflate geometric qualities with moral ones. Aldous Huxley called the straight line "the geometrical symbol of triumphant human purpose." Straight as an arrow. The straight and narrow. A straight shooter. Straightforward. (To say nothing about "straight" as the normative sexual category.)

Meanwhile, as anthropologist Tim Ingold has noted, there is no lack of metaphors in the English language for that which is *not* straight: "There is the twisted mind of the pervert, the crooked mind of the criminal, the devious mind of the swindler and the wandering mind of the idiot."

The phrase "straight and narrow" comes from a misunderstanding of Matthew 7:13–14 (and Luke 13:24) of the King James (Authorized) translation of the Bible. As Jesus tells it, while "wide is the gate, and broad is the way, that leadeth to destruction, . . . strait is the gate and narrow is the way, which leadeth unto life, and few there be that find it." The word *strait* is a synonym for *narrow*, and Jesus was using the age-old rhetorical device of saying the same thing in two different ways for emphasis. The alteration to *straight* in the idiom happened around 1930, as the Depression was deepening.

---

were leveled to create straight, well-organized streets. Representative of these changes, New York City under the Commissioners' Plan of 1811 set about instituting a grid system. In 1853, Paris under Napoléon III instituted the Haussmann Plan, which created Paris's wide and beautifully imperious boulevards, gardens, and squares. These wide streets were meant to make the city more livable, but as critics noted, they also made it easier to move armies through the streets in order to control social unrest. Other cities followed suit. Linearity, the thinking was, represented beauty, uniformity, rationality, and above all else, order.

Street by street, sidewalks were built to separate walkers from traffic and keep them walking in a straight line. Police forces were commissioned to make sure order was maintained, to "keep people in line." Public schools were created to keep children from being idle in the streets and to prepare them for a lifetime of work. Efforts were made to take commerce out of the streets and into shops and department stores. Mass public transportation systems meant that workers could be shunted out into the suburbs, spreading thin (or at least thinner) the population, reducing the opportunities to riot. With each of these adaptations to the city (the shops, the schools, the prisons, the public transportation), queueing became more and more the norm.

In these newly modernized cities, queues are formed by a variety of tactics. Some of these are voluntary, as Stanley

Milgram noted. Others are more coercive. Of the latter sort, we find the turnstile, the velvet rope, the police barricade, and other sundry herding devices. An early example was the barrier often seen at the entrances of France's libraries, schools, and theaters. This was the architectural solution to English pushing and shoving advocated by the correspondent to *The Builder*, mentioned above.

"Instead of being allowed to block up the doorway indiscriminately," he wrote, "visitors are obliged to stand in file between barriers made along the walls for the purpose. . . . As there is only room for one person, or at most for two persons abreast, it is evidently out of the question to obtain a more advanced position by pushing between those in front (such pushing in France would be resented as an affront), and therefore every one keeps quietly in his place, and follows those in front as fast as they are admitted." He could see no reason for England not to implement "the public form 'la queue' at railway booking offices . . . at theatres, and wherever a crowd is expected."

But as city planners soon found out, there are also less noticeably coercive ways to get the scrum to form orderly lines. A good example is the 1899 redesign of the Grand Central Depot into the Grand Central Terminal in New York City, through which millions of people filter weekly.

The idea behind the original Depot was that it would help control the behavior of the crowd by marking a transition space between the rough-and-tumble sorts of crowd behavior one experiences out in the street and the sort of crowd behavior one would like near a large, fast-moving, and possibly fatal piece of machinery. The stately, awe-inspiring, cathedral-like Beaux Arts building was supposed to signal that a certain solemnity of purpose was expected of the traveler. The message was: "Crowd, tame thyself."

Did it work? God, no. It takes more than the bigness and beauty of architecture to get a crowd to behave itself. As one witness complained, passengers "are passed in like hogs. Just before the train starts—sometimes only ten minutes, the doors are opened and there is a scramble pell-mell. Hats are knocked off, people kicked in the shins, trampled on the toes and pushed this way and that. I have seen women treated shamefully in that way. I have known them to be left behind for two trains after they have been waiting a whole hour, but could not get through the gate." The depot was mainly just a large open space; there were no spatial cues for how or where to move. Only months after it was constructed, it was deemed a public nuisance.

The redesign into the Grand Central Terminal, then, sought to direct the crowd, and it did so by crafting a deliberately choreographed experience for the traveler. No longer would the passenger simply enter the depot as into an arena, gladiator spear in hand; with the redesign, he would be herded individually through an elegant system of corridors, concourses, ramps, tunnels, and gates, synchronized by the opening and closing of certain arteries of circulation according to clocks that were everywhere in the terminal. Moreover, operations within the terminal were centralized. Before, each passenger would have dealt with individual rail companies; now there was a ticketing desk the same for all—first come, first served (FCFS). The designers created separate waiting areas for immigrants, so that they wouldn't disrupt the normative codes of conduct.

They wanted the crowd as homogeneous, as anonymous, as possible; the crowd would behave as clockwork mechanisms. The designers of the Grand Central Terminal were seeking, in short, to create the sort of city dweller Stanley Milgram described in "The Experience of Living in Cities." Apparently, the redesign worked wonderfully.

Everyone (who was not an immigrant) would share the same experience at the same point in their journey, but sequentially, spread out, one at a time, face-to-back, alone, aloof. In line. At all points, the traveler would be reminded that she was an individual—an individual who behaves,

From the Annals of Line Standing

In 1916, Clarence Saunders opened Piggly Wiggly, America's first fully self-service grocery store, in Memphis, Tennessee. It would revolutionize the way Americans shop for food. From pictures of this early store, however, we see that Saunders didn't have very much faith that the average customer would know how to queue properly.

To my eyes, the grocery store resembles a tiny little prison (truly minuscule by the standards of today's behemoth supermarkets). Customers entered one at a time through a turnstile. Once inside, chain-link fences on either side of the turnstile prevented them from escaping. They would be led ineluctably down a maze of short, narrow aisles, in which they passed each and every product for sale in turn (no skipping an aisle!). At the end of the maze, the customer wound up at the cashier desk, which was itself surrounded by a wooden queue barrier, spaced tightly enough to ensure that no one could squeeze past the person in front (tight enough that I wonder whether it would accommodate the growing waistlines of Americans in the decades to follow). On the way out, the customer passed through a separate turnstile, and then—at last—would be free to behave as disorderly as she pleased.

somewhat paradoxically, like all other individuals—despite being part of a crowd. Such is the ideal citizen.

THE MACHINE-MADE MAN

The birth of the queue, it seems, came about through a confluence of forces. Waiting is as old as wanting, and so is forming mobs. But how we wait isn't. And grateful as I am that people don't push and shove when I'm trying to get on the subway, I wonder: What have we lost as part of the bargain?

When René Clair directed his wonderful musical slapstick *À Nous la Liberté* (Freedom for Us) in 1931, he used the comedically choreographed military precision of the lines within the modern automated factory—itself exaggeratedly shiny, spotless, ultramodern, immense, and comically high-tech, done up in the high rectilinear style of Art Deco—to suggest that the workers had become as much machines as men. The escaped prisoners who find themselves working in this factory simply find themselves in a new type of prison. The physical comedy comes out of the inability of the two prisoners to adapt themselves to this machine.

Recently I watched the late onetime U.S. Poet Laureate Philip Levine give an interview to Bill Moyers on PBS.

He was explaining the inspiration behind his poem "What Work Is." The poem begins:

> *We stand in the rain in a long line*
> *waiting at Ford Highland Park. For work.*
> *You know what work is—if you're*
> *old enough to read this you know what*
> *work is, although you may not do it.*
> *Forget you. This is about waiting,*
> *shifting from one foot to another.*

In his interview, Levine—who spent much of his early life working assembly lines in Detroit—recalls the bitter memory of being made to wait for two hours in line for the Employment Office to open. The office was supposed to open at eight a.m., but instead it opened at ten. As in the poem, he remembers it raining.

"And I like a jerk stayed," Levine tells Moyers. "All those two hours. I kept thinking, 'Well it opens soon. It'll open—.' No. We all stood there. And then I realized they want those of us who are willing to stand two hours in the rain. They want to hire us. They know how docile we are already. We just proved it to them. We'll take any kind of crap they dish out, right?" What does the queue represent to Levine? Docility. Men who have been broken of their spirit.

I have not yet mentioned the role schools play in the birth of the queue and in its upkeep as a cultural form. Training for a life of line standing begins early, and if you don't believe me, recall the sweat that goes into teaching rambunctious kindergartners to pipe down, take turns, and line up already. Teaching manuals offer teachers exercises in how to get children to queue properly. Children are taught to speak in turn, not to cut in line. They are apportioned belongings (a desk, pencils, crayons) and given grades: this teaches them to think of themselves as separate individuals, not as members of a crowd. They are taught to mind the strictures of the clock—to obey the clock—which orders every part of their day. They are taught the torturous task of working through their boredom now that their time no longer belongs to them.

One could argue that this is the real formative training of grade school. And I do think that it's important to teach children the value of equality, good behavior, patience, and hard work. But sometimes I wonder: Are we simply teaching them to be compliant, passive, docile? I think to some degree the answer is yes.

I was surprised to find that such a sentiment had been expressed as long ago as 1891, a time when some people could presumably still remember a time before the ubiquity of lines. That was the year that Congressman George Cooper of Indiana stood up to deliver a eulogy for recently departed Congressman Frank Spinola of New York. As a side note, he bemoaned the alienation of modern life that finds its synecdoche in line standing.

"At the doorway of our schools," he said, "the children stand in line; having entered they are graded and classified, and the necessity for discipline and methods in dealing with numbers leaves little room for the orderly exercise or development of individual traits. Instead of dealing with the child as a plant which should be suffered to develop on all sides in obedience to the law of its nature and from the forces supplied from within, it is set in a row and trimmed so that the lines be even the general effect symmetrical."

From school, they would go on to a lifetime of similar passivity in the queue. "Men must stand in line at the shop, at the ticket office at the theater, at the railway station, and even at the doors of our popular churches," Cooper said. "The village blacksmith now stands among a wilderness of wheels, where he is known by number and not by name, and merely superintends a machine which is in itself almost automatic. Our Priscilla is taken from her spindle and her distaff, and she stands in line to watch the play of steam-driven fingers."

The conditions in the city of the nineteenth century (or in a classroom without discipline) sound like a chore, granted. But who could say of any group shuffling their way through an airport screening that they are, as Carlyle said of the French mob, "rapid, audacious; so clear-sighted, inventive, prompt to seize the moment; instinct with life to its finger-ends"? He could be describing children before they are put through the American public school system. Whatever happened to people like that? (The news suggests to me they may be in Tunisia, Cairo, Syria, Istanbul, Buenos Aires.)

Congressman Cooper characterized the age he lived in as that of "Machine-Made Men." (Are we any less so now?) He identified the late Congressman Spinola as one of the last non-machine-made men. That would make him special indeed. We may never see his like again. May he rest in peace.

CHAPTER THREE

A STATIONARY STATE OF MIND
On the Psychology of Waiting

A robot that stands in line is a commonplace of science fiction: Everyone knows that in the future nearly all aspects of people's jobs, homes, and lives will be outsourced to robots. When the price is right, a machine-made man is fairly easily replaced by machine. And standing in line? Perhaps that too. You'll know you've arrived in the future when there's a robot in front of you at Starbucks, patiently waiting to place an order. Though he never used the word, Stanley Milgram (among others) suggested that mankind in the metropolitan environment becomes more robotic (mechanical, impersonal, task-oriented). So why not go the last step, and simply build a line-standing robot?

Such a future is not as far away as you think. It's not even in the future. In fact, that particular robot was invented over twenty years ago, and his name is Xavier. He was constructed in 1995 by a team at the Robotics Institute at Carnegie Mellon University. Xavier is cylindrical, two feet in diameter and stands about waist high. He moves around on hidden wheels and sees through a pair of stereoscopic cameras mounted to his top. If R2D2 ever made love to a garbage disposal unit, their offspring might look a little like him.

His creators call him a social robot, programmed to autonomously do a variety of "social" things (including wandering around from cubicle to cubicle telling robot-themed knock-knock jokes, like that one coworker in the office who never seems to do any work). One of these tasks was standing in line at the coffee shop in the building where the Robotics Institute is located, where he would order a coffee.

When a person (or a robot) stands in line, she makes a series of decisions reacting to the environment around her, some not always entirely conscious. These decisions are not unlike the ones a computer program algorithmically makes by design: If A, then B.

Scan the area. Is there more than one line? Then join what you perceive to be the shortest of them. Is the line too long? Then don't join it (a move researchers call *balking*). Is there a well-ordered line? Then line up. Is there a disorganized line? Then stand in such a position to the people in front of you that someone coming later will recognize that you are waiting. If you join a line, give enough personal space to the people around you, but not so much personal space that someone might cut in front of you. If someone looks you in the eye, then look down at your shoes. If the person in front of you steps forward, then you step forward too. If someone cuts in front of you, give him hell. If the wait takes too long (based on some internal calculation of cost versus reward), then you might even decide to step out of line (researchers call this *reneging*). Et cetera.

You might say each of us has been programmed to make these decisions, based on a murky combination of culture, individual circumstances, and personality. For a robot, all of these microdecisions must be made explicit; otherwise it won't know what to do. There are many challenges in training a robot to queue. How close does a robot stand in proximity to the people around it? How does a robot even recognize that a given group of people are forming a queue (not something always easy for humans to discern)? Or for that matter, how does a robot even recognize a human as such, to make sure it's not lining up behind, say, a lamppost, a garbage can, an ATM?

Like a piece on a game board, Xavier takes the queue step-by-step, according to the algorithmic rules he was set up with. He goes into the situation knowing only a few things. He knows where the barista is (the "point of service"). He can recognize which people are in line, using a "person-detection algorithm" that also determines their body orientation (they are generally facing forward). He also knows the levels of personal space people standing in line expect, which both helps him determine which people are in line (and not just a random bystander), and tells him how close to stand next to the person in front of him. His creators determined American personal space by standing in line themselves, and testing for distances that made them uncomfortable, which they turned into an average for Xavier to follow.

To determine where the back of the line is, Xavier moves backward from the front, parallel to the line. He stops and takes a scan of the person at the head, who is ordering a coffee. Xavier moves back a space, takes another scan of the second person in line. Repeat. He does this until he makes a scan, and there's no person there. He has found the end of the line. He moves in. He continues to scan the people in front of him. If the person ahead of him steps forward, he does too. Repeat, until what he scans isn't the back of someone's legs, but the flat smooth service counter.

He puts the coffee on his tab, thanks the barista, and returns the coffee to the person who ordered it. Mission accomplished.

Xavier correctly stood in line 70 percent of the time. Occasionally he got the shape of the line wrong, standing behind someone who was only line-adjacent. He could handle a slightly curved line, but if the line bent too sharply, he got lost. Sometimes something about a person's haircut (up-dos in particular, for whatever reason) caused him to miscalculate personal space. He was decidedly slow to assess the situation, having to stop and scan each time before deciding the next step. But overall, not bad. He did better than some people I've encountered in the wild.

His creators were pleased to note that several people got in line behind Xavier, which they cited as "anecdotal evidence that Xavier is considered, in some sense, to be a social member of the community." I imagine that the Robotics Institute must be a surreal place to work sometimes.

KEEP CALM AND CARRY ON

Maybe it's just as well for a robot to take over our line-standing duties. We humans have never really been ideally suited to the task.

The experiment with Xavier not only represents progress in the field of "social" robotics, but by comparing his own relatively simple decision-making process to our own, we see how complex ours really is. Of course, Xavier was lucky to queue in a social space where lines are short and generally easy to read, and even then he made it through only 70 percent of the time. In real life, we are constantly encountering situations where order isn't so neatly determined. When Xavier encountered a queueing situation that was not addressed explicitly in his program, he stalled. When humans encounter a queueing situation outside our personal and cultural expectations (our own programming), we become dumb and anxious. In extreme cases, sometimes we stall too.

As far as social conventions like line standing go, humans aspire to (and often fall short of) the condition of robot. Call this the principle of mental energy conservation: We want to expend only as little brainpower as is necessary to live. Thinking burns calories. Our bodies tell us to conserve calories. A queue is a simple, easy-to-understand social construction that (while far from perfect, as we'll see) is generally a fair way of distributing limited resources, one that allows us not to think too hard.

Mental energy conservation explains a lot. If given the choice, I believe most people would choose the tightly regulated line with well-defined boundaries over the looser slightly disorganized one, because constantly looking over your shoulder to ensure your place requires thinking, however marginal the threat. In addition, the vast majority of people don't try to cut in line because that would simply require more work (the time it takes to poach a spot, the possibility that one might get into an altercation, and the need to create an alibi for why you need to cut in line all sound exhausting to me).

This, at least, is the conclusion Stanley Milgram came to in the 1980s, when he conducted a pair of experiments in which he and a group of his graduate students went through crowded New York City subway cars asking strangers to give up their seats (rightfully theirs according to the principle of first come, first served). Later, he sent the same students out to cut in line at ticket counters, to see if the results would be similar. In both cases, they gave no reason for their intrusion.

The findings surprised Milgram. First, people actually were willing to give up their seats about 50 percent of the time. Around the same percentage put up no protest when the graduate students cut in line, but when people did put up a stink, they put up a more visible stink (a mixture of physical action, loud verbal refusal, and dirty looks). But half the time? Nada. No response.

But what was almost more interesting was the personal

effect the exercise had on Milgram and his graduate students: They all found the experience to be utterly exhausting emotionally. They were anxious, sweaty, embarrassed. Milgram characterized the experience as "wrenching." Why didn't more New Yorkers put up a fuss to these impertinent line cutters? Why did Milgram and his students feel so anxious doing it? Their reactions greatly exceeded the scope of their transgression. Most of the people who had been transgressed didn't even object. What gives?

What it comes down to, Milgram argued, is social cost. When a certain practice becomes a social convention (recognized universally within a community), you must do more work to explain why you get to flout it. When a high-enough percentage of people within a community recognize first come, first served as the social norm, and you don't want to stand in line, you have the burden of proof in convincing them you deserve to cut in. If there's a compelling reason why you would expend so much energy, perhaps due to an emergency, people will indeed often give way. If it's not an emergency, be willing to defend yourself against verbal (or sometimes physical) attack. And then you might simply be sent to the back of the line, and your little misadventure in cutting in has cost you that much more time.

Meanwhile, roughly half the people whom Milgram and his students cut in front of didn't say a word. Milgram believed that this also has to do with cost. The first person to be cut in front of is the most likely to complain, partly because he would have the clearest view of the incursion, and partly because he has the most to lose, at least in terms of percentage of his time. (For instance, if there are ten people in line, and the line-cutter cuts in front of everyone, the extra cost in terms of time for the person immediately after the line cutter doubles, but for the tenth person in line, the cost increases by only 10 percent.) But it also costs him least to protest, because he doesn't need to step out of line to do so. At the same time, he might wonder whether it's worth complaining, when he's nearly at the front of the line himself.

And say you are several people behind the line cutter. To protest, you have to get out of line to say something to him. To do so, you risk your own place in line. If enough people protest, the line wavers and threatens to dissolve. People tolerate line cutters because to do so puts the queue at risk at the cost of a single person. You might be annoyed by the transgression, but to say something would cost you more energy than it's worth. The more people who cut, however, the more likely you are to complain, because that constitutes a less tolerable cost. Milgram viewed this ability of line standers to tolerate line cutters as part of the health and stability of the queue: It can withstand incursions, because "a system's resilience depends not only on its capacity to defend against disturbances, but also its capacity to ignore, adjust to, and tolerate them." We feel threatened more by the possibility of disorder than by a single line cutter.

A good place to view this sort of behavior, actually, is in traffic, where one lane has to merge into another lane (a form of queueing). In my home state of Minnesota, the Department of Transportation is currently plastering the roads with billboards asking drivers to stop being so "Minnesota nice" on the road (we are a ridiculously polite bunch, it's true). In particular, the DOT wants us all to become "late mergers." The vehicular version of line-cutters, in other words. When drivers merge late, they use the freeway more efficiently: If everyone merges early three miles down from the bottleneck, that's three miles of road that isn't being used, a not very efficient use of freeway. According to the DOT, doing so "will reduce the length of the backup by up to 50%," making wait times for everyone shorter. The DOT also claims such a system makes traffic safer, because it means that there won't be two separate lanes moving at drastically different speeds. We will *all* be better off if we allow others to "zipper in."

Do I do this? Of course not. I merge early like everyone who isn't a thoughtless jerk. Yes, but . . . I want to say when I'm stuck in the slow lane for an eternity, in conversation with the DOT billboard ahead of me. Is it fair? Here I am, being a considerate driver, and I'm supposed to let this asshole who waited until the last second to merge get to his destination ahead of me?

But the truth is, the real reason I merge early is that I don't want to go through the hassle of trying to squeeze in farther down the road and look like an asshole myself. There's more certainty involved in merging early and thus less stress. It costs me less psychologically to do so. Meanwhile, my response (usually) to the guy who does follow the DOT's recommendation, and noses in at the last moment, is to finally let him in with a resigned sigh: *Well, if you want that extra minute so bad, asshole. . . .* I let it go, because the other driver simply isn't worth the emotional investment of being angry. That doesn't mean I'm happy about it.

WWXD? What would Xavier do? Depends on whether he was programmed to be sociable or efficient. His agility in getting to the coffee counter is secondary to his ability to stand in line, and so he'd probably merge early (because that's the sociable thing to do). On the other hand, there's a more recent line-standing robot (in a sense) that would merge late: Google's Self-Driving Car, which takes people

Rage Against the Machine

The familiar phenomenon known as road rage has its cousin in queue or line rage, both born out of similar feelings of frustration and anxiety, typified by outbursts of verbal and sometimes physical aggression.

SHOPPER DEAD AFTER "QUEUE RAGE" ATTACK (Metro.co.uk, News, June 12, 2008).

MARSHALS BROUGHT IN TO STOP LATE NIGHT TAXI QUEUE RAGE (*The News,* January 18, 2010).

BURGER-RAGE MUM ATTACKED WOMEN AT DRIVE-THROUGH MCDONALD'S QUEUE IN SALFORD (*Manchester Evening News,* March 2, 2012).

There are dozens of examples of line rage in the news. (It's interesting that most of them are reported by British news services, casting doubts on the notion of patient British queuer.) And these are simply the examples of those in which police had to become involved. Whether or not we've physically assaulted anyone over some indiscretion of line etiquette, I think many of us have reacted in sometimes aggressively unkind ways in our frustration, speaking angrily to either a fellow line stander or to our service provider. I still feel a little embarrassed about the way I once spoke to a Comcast representative, after an hour-long wait at one of the company's offices. I should have blamed the upper levels of the corporation—and the monopoly Comcast holds in many areas of the country—not the poor underlings who work for them. Queues can be so frustrating that sometimes we simply feel the need—deep down, instinctually—to fight. And afterward, for many of us, to regret fighting.

There's at least one writer who has contemplated a world in which these sorts of assaults are not only justified but encouraged—the revered science fiction author Robert Heinlein (probably most famous for *Starship Troopers*). On the planet of Tellus Tertius, represented in the book *The Cat Who Walks Through Walls*, shooting a line cutter on the spot is considered an act of justifiable homicide (or rather "homicide in the public interest"). In the novel, this is what happens to a "rancid tourist from Secundus." The shooter is found innocent of all guilt. The character who tells the story—who did not do the shooting herself—admits that she believes the choice to slay the tourist was a bit "drastic"; she herself always responds to line cutters with only "minor mayhem," such as breaking the offender's arm. But otherwise, she shrugs off the killing. It's an example less of rage, I suppose, than of cold-blooded, officially sanctioned murder, but I wager it would teach people a lesson!

---

out of the equation altogether. Reduced traffic congestion is just one of the myriad benefits of removing the driver from the driver's seat.

When the Self-Driving Car zippers in at that last second, the person inside can only shrug at the other driver: What can I do? I'm not making the decisions around here. There's nothing else you can say.

SLIPS AND SKIPS

On the other hand, sometimes cutting in line costs little or nothing in terms of mental energy conservation. The social rules begrudgingly allow it. You have nothing to defend yourself against. This is the case when the grocery store opens up a new lane, and you're the lucky bastard in the right place and the right time.

This is a case of "slips and skips," according to Dr. Richard Larson, a professor of operations research at MIT and probably the world's foremost authority on the subject of queueing. He calls himself Dr. Queue. The name makes him sound like a costumed comic book character. Appropriately enough, he has an origins story to match.

Operations research can generally be a fairly wonky field of science. Researchers crunch numbers about operations large and small to determine how to increase their efficiency. Need to shave off minutes getting that hamburger into the hands of the consumer? Need to simplify your global supply chains to keep costs down? Run the models. Do the math. What operations research normally doesn't take into account, however, is how customers feel about the experience. Where does an understanding of consumer psychology come into play?

Dr. Queue began thinking about consumer psychology following an incident at a department store. He was waiting at the inventory window to pick up a bicycle he had bought for his son. He stood there for thirty-five minutes. "I watched numerous customers," he writes, "successfully pick up their waffle irons, quilts, or automatic coffee makers and leave the store, typically within several minutes after arriving at the check-out window." But not him. On his way out to the car, he was seething. He vowed to return the bike the next day. He would give his business to someone who better deserved it.

It's completely possible that from the department store's perspective, their method of delivering goods was an efficient one (or at least more so than alternative methods). But it didn't take into account what it felt like for the consumer on the losing end of that arrangement. Operations research, Dr. Queue felt, had to take that into consideration too.

What Dr. Queue experienced that day was a *skip*. He was being skipped over by other consumers. When the grocery store opens a new checkout lane, it's irritating when a person who was behind you in line now gets to check out ahead of you. The social convention that's supposed to cause you less stress is now causing you more stress.

Meanwhile, if you're the person who benefits from that new lane being opened, likely you don't feel any guilt whatsoever. On the contrary, you would thank your good fortune. The people who walked out promptly with their toasters and waffle irons were probably simply thankful that they didn't have to wait like that poor schmuck waiting for his son's bicycle. The universe was going their way, because they experienced a *slip*. The system allowed them to slip in in front of him.

Slips and skips: two separate mental reactions to the same phenomenon. This isn't the case of someone deliberately cutting in front of you in line. After all, you can't blame a person for doing something that you would do if you were in her shoes. You know how the game works: That person doesn't have to explain anything. But slips and skips violate the egalitarian spirit of queueing. You stand in line precisely because you don't want to think too hard to get what's fair. But when the grocery store opens that other lane, you have to start jockeying for position again. Not fair! The trade-off was for naught.

This is why a study comparing the service of three different fast-food chains, McDonald's, Burger King, and

Wendy's, determined that while McDonald's and Burger King had much quicker service, customers were on the whole much more satisfied with the service at Wendy's. Why? Because Wendy's is the only one of the three that guarantees service in the order customers arrive in, using a queue barrier. (Dave Thomas, the company's founder, had a long-standing hatred of uneven wait times, according to company lore.) Likewise, a recent study has shown that grocery stores could dramatically increase customer satisfaction by introducing a single-file system. No more of that emotionally fraught exercise of hunting down what you perceive to be the shortest line, and feeling frustrated when the other lines move faster than yours.

The downside? This would probably slow down operations as a whole. People would wait longer on the whole to get their groceries to checkout. The upside? People would experience the wait as shorter. (People aren't all that good at objectively measuring their own misery, it turns out.) By opening that new lane, the grocery store was simply trying to shorten wait times. But it actually works against them in the eyes of the public. As Dr. Queue warns, companies ignore customer psychology at their peril. When one person enjoys a slip, many more customers behind him experience a skip. The problem is, they blame the grocery store, not the slipper.

Americans value efficiency, it's true. But like Xavier, they are programmed first and foremost as social robots, and to be social is to wait your turn.

OPERATION ENDURE

Xavier is lucky on another count, as well: His brain (so to speak) was programmed to do one thing and one thing only: wait in line, and order a coffee. He would be perfectly content to wait in line until either his order was fulfilled or his batteries ran dry. If only we humans could be so single-minded too. Wouldn't it be nice to have a switch to turn off the parts of our brain not currently needed for the task at hand? I think life would run more smoothly that way.

To stand in line is to put yourself at the mercy of others. You are relying on other people to feed you, to clothe you. That itself is enough to make a person feel vulnerable. You volunteer to put yourself into this holding pattern—this imaginary box—for X amount of time, and at the end you walk away with a television, a toaster oven, the DVD set of *Storage Wars* season 5. You only have a binary option: Stay in line or get out of line. That's it. Meanwhile, your brain is decidedly not like Xavier's. It's not all that dissimilar from the one your caveman ancestors had, and it runs in all directions at once. You feel trapped as a result.

I personally can't think of another social situation that so regularly and so reliably induces at least some small level of anxiety. Why is there only one cashier when there's a line out the door? There's no line, so how do I know who goes next? Am I next? When is this going to end? Why is that line going faster than mine? Who has right-of-way here? Oh no, the little old lady ahead of me is paying for groceries *with coupons and a personal check! Who still does that?* An internal mini tsunami siren goes off in my head. *Danger! Danger! Fight or flight?* (I exaggerate only somewhat.) These panicky thoughts are usually momentary, but rarely (if ever) rational. The concern I felt at the time always seems a little silly in retrospect.

Sometimes these feelings manifest themselves as problems in extreme cases, like that of a friend of mine for whom standing in line too long is a trigger causing bladder problems. She carries around a doctor's note explaining that, no, she really can't wait! Psychiatrists call this "situational anxiety," which in this case is not unlike claustrophobia. Nearly everyone feels (and fears) being trapped sometimes, to some extent. For some, this becomes a phobia; for most others, just a trivial but real daily annoyance. When the wait time is excessive, the social convention that was supposed to conserve mental energy becomes the focus of a great deal of mental energy. Line standing is

The Lame Shall Walk

Could anxiety account for the high number of cases of temporary bodily ailments witnessed in airport lines? Airport personnel could tell you about this strange phenomenon: the traveler who must be pushed to the front of the line in a wheelchair, and once through—what magic is this?—is healed instantaneously of his ailment. A miracle. As Jesus told the lame man, "Get up, pick up your suitcase, and walk to your boarding gate." The number of people who enter in wheelchairs exceed the number who leave in wheelchairs.

Are these cases of hysterical paralysis, cured as soon as the ordeal is over? Doubtful. More likely they are people exploiting a loophole, in order to cut in line. Airport employees cannot demand travelers tell them about their confidential medical histories, so there's nothing stopping those travelers from getting into a wheelchair and being escorted through the priority queue.

People in wheelchairs must also be boarded onto the airplane first. Especially for flights to certain areas of the world—Egypt, the Philippines, Boca Raton—there might be a dozen people waiting in wheelchairs. Then, at their destination, the wheelchair pushers waiting for their appointed travelers find that they've already walked off the plane on their own two feet. People in wheelchairs board first (good), but disembark last (bad). How convenient, then, that by the end of the flight they appear to be cured. Flight attendants call these "miracle flights."

It isn't just airports that experience these sorts of line-standing shenanigans. Disneyland, for instance, recently had to make revisions to its Guest Assistance Card (GAC) program, which allows people with disabilities priority queueing rights. Because they too don't require proof of disability, they also frequently get guests who look suspiciously able-bodied for needing assistance.

More nefarious still are the reports of wealthy people hiring black-market "tour concierges" at Disneyland, people with disabilities (or at least people who claim to have disabilities) who pose as family members in order to get everyone in through the back door. According to the *New York Post* and a separate undercover investigation by NBC News in Los Angeles, these concierges charge anywhere from $50 an hour to $200 an hour. In response to these allegations of exploitation, in 2013 Disney disbanded their GAC program, replacing it with a new program meant to be more equitable to everyone. Instead of giving disabled guests immediate access to rides, they have to make an appointment based on ride wait times, not unlike Disney's FastPass system, which is available to everyone. This, Disney claims, will discourage abuse of the system while continuing to ease the burden of their genuinely disabled guests.

As Jesus also told the lame man, "Go and sin no more."

supposed to free you to think about other things instead, but in time, all you can think about is the fact that you're not really moving anywhere.

In 1985, David Maister, a well-regarded business management consultant and professor at the Harvard Business School, published an influential article titled "The Psychology of Waiting Lines," warning of the dangers of businesses giving people like me (namely, just about everyone) too much free rein to indulge our anxieties. We pose a problem for businesses. Businesses can't always improve their wait times. Sometimes they wouldn't want to even if they could. The economic model of a theme park, for instance, depends on people waiting to get on a ride; otherwise they will have exhausted all the possibilities of the park in an hour or two.

Queues in a modern economy are inevitable, but they have the power to significantly sour a customer's attitude toward a place. There's a certain coffee shop and bakery in my neighborhood that's a lovely place to hang out, but I increasingly refuse to go there because to do so is always a gamble. The cramped, crowded wait takes as much as ten minutes sometimes, and there's never enough personnel handling the orders. *But all I want is a simple black coffee!* I want to cry from the back of the line, shifting my weight impatiently from foot to foot. *I have exact change!* Xavier would handle the situation with far more grace than I can ever seem to manage.

From the Annals of Line Standing

We know this much: At least once in human history someone has bought an admission ticket simply for the sake of standing in a line. This was the case when the Manhattan Savings Bank discovered a person selling admission tickets to stand in its bank-teller lines. (Bank guards quickly gave the scalper the boot.)

Why were the Manhattan Savings Bank teller lines so popular? As a way of distracting people from the fact that they are waiting, the bank began offering entertainment. Its managers hired world-class concert pianists to serenade people while they waited between 10:00 a.m. and 2:00 p.m., their peak hours. In time, this lunch concert became so popular that people began coming just for the sake of the music (and later other forms of entertainment, such as dog shows and even a small bank-lobby version of Christmas on Ice).

According to Richard Larson (Dr. Queue), the Manhattan Savings Bank (which no longer exists, due to a bank merger in 1990) is a model for ways that companies can transform wasted, empty, unoccupied time, into socially uplifting occupied time.

But is the line at my coffee shop really ten minutes? I've never actually timed my ordeal, but it certainly feels like ten minutes. And according to Maister, that's really what's important to customers. People are not great at thinking objectively about the passage of time when they are in captivity. Time is subjective, and we perceive it to be moving more slowly when we're standing still. A company can make the time seem to pass more slowly, as by letting others skip ahead. But by the same token, it has an opportunity to make time seem to pass more quickly. Why fix the problem, Maister argues, when you can fix the perception of the problem? That's mostly what people care about anyway.

The trick is either to distract the customer from the fact that she is waiting or to adopt a series of tactics that make her feel more in control of her own circumstance. For instance, there is something particularly agonizing about being put on hold on the phone. In most situations, you neither know how long your wait will last, nor can you come to a rough guesstimate based on a visual scan of the number of people in line. A person might walk into the store, do a double take at the line, do a quick cost/benefit analysis (*Nope. No way. Not now.*) and go home. On the phone, you are blind. You could be the next caller, or you could be the hundredth caller. It's a terrible feeling. You feel trapped. The wait takes an eternity as a result.

David Maister's Eight Propositions Concerning the Psychology of Waiting

1. Occupied Time Feels Shorter Than Unoccupied Time. This one seems obvious, captured in that pithy maxim "A watched pot never boils." Distraction is key. Get a subscription to *National Geographic* for your waiting room. Let diners wait in the bar until a table clears up. If possible, give them some task related to what they came for, like providing a medical history form to fill out. The reason?—

2. People Want to Get Started. An initial check in point, like a restaurant hostess who takes down your name for the next available table, puts people at ease; the wait feels shorter as a result. The business recognizes they are there; they are "in the system" and so don't have to worry so much (the same reason why most people merge early in traffic). The message is: "We know you're here, and we're doing everything to get you seated." Why does the wait after check-in feel shorter? Because . . .

3. Anxiety Makes Waits Seem Longer. When a person is in line, there are so many uncertainties. When will the line end? Why did that guy get his order before I did? Will there be a seat for me on the bus? In line, a person no longer feels in charge of a situation. We become all the more conscious of the fact that we're waiting. The more companies are able to relieve these uncertainties, the shorter the wait will feel, because . . .

4. Uncertain Waits Are Longer Than Known, Finite Waits. Few things make a person feel more powerless than having no idea when the wait will end. We feel more in control of the situation when we have an estimated time of service. You think, *A five-minute wait? Yeah, I guess I can do a five-minute wait.* For this reason, some major cities now post expected travel times during rush hour, and at the deli you can check your take-a-ticket number against the number being called out. That's only two numbers before mine? Well I guess that shouldn't take too long.

5. Unexplained Waits Are Longer Than Explained Waits. When traffic gets backed up too long, I sometimes have a highly uncharitable thought: There'd better be a crash up ahead with a considerable body count to warrant this mess. Once I can see the reason for the backup (a lane closure, for instance), I almost always immediately relax. A story (correct or not) helps make line standers feel less vulnerable in a situation they are powerless to remedy. We feel better when we know why our flight has been delayed. And the business had better give a reason (any reason) for the delay, lest the customer create his own, less charitable story to post on Yelp.

6. Unfair Waits Are Longer Than Equitable Waits. Slips and skips. Did the person who entered the adjacent checkout line get to their cashier quicker? Are the first-class ticket holders boarding, while you're back in the coach-seat-ticket-holding scrum? Did the table who ordered after you get their meal before yours? Even when such violations of the first in, first out principle are warranted—a dying person gets priority in the ER, for instance—they only aggravate your sense of how long you've waited.

7. The More Valuable the Service, the Longer the Customer Will Wait. If—for whatever reason—I'm away from my coffeepot in the morning and desperately need coffee, I will not hesitate to wait a good ten to fifteen minutes at Starbucks, if that's what it takes. If I'm just looking for an optional midafternoon caffeinated pick-me-up, on the other hand, there'd better not be more than three or four people in front of me, tops, or I'm outta there. This is why grocery stores have express lanes, as people with fewer items in their basket are more likely to balk when they see the wait. Meanwhile, companies that are virtual monopolies (telecom providers, I'm looking at you) don't have to give a crap about wait times, because what's a person supposed to do? Go without Internet? No wonder, then, that Internet providers have a lower customer satisfaction rating than any other industry.

8. Solo Waits Feel Longer Than Group Waits. Where lines are long and unavoidable, get people talking. Where possible, companies should foster a sense of community. They might complain or joke about the wait, but at least they aren't solemnly brooding alone about the evanescence of a wasted life spent standing in line. This doesn't mean that the line will exactly feel like a party, but from personal experience I can attest to the sense of togetherness that sometimes develops with the strangers around you in line. We become a little band of survivors, with a grim gallows humor to match. We're all in this thing together.

In his tract, David Maister proposed eight theories concerning the psychology of line standers (many of them subsequently confirmed by researchers like Dr. Queue), and in the last decade or so, you can begin to see some of them in action. Lately I've noticed that telephone queues often feature a callback option, in which the company calls you when the queue has subsided. Sometimes a human voice will periodically punctuate the endless public domain smooth jazz coming out of your headset: "There are two callers ahead of you," she says. When I hear her sweet, sweet voice, I immediately feel less tense. I have a rough estimate of how long I'll wait. I feel I'm in control of the situation (even though I'm not really). The company cares that I'm waiting here miserably with a telephone glued to my ear.

Dr. Queue gives examples of even simpler fixes. Some years ago, the Houston airport began getting flooded with complaints about how long baggage claims took. What did they do? They simply increased the distance between the terminal and the baggage carousel, making travelers walk farther to get their luggage. Complaints fell away to zero—problem solved. Everyone's happy.

Another: Ever notice that there's almost always a mirror next to the elevator you're waiting for? Thank some genius working in an early Manhattan skyscraper for that. When management began getting complaints about how slow their elevators were, they couldn't exactly tear out their elevators and begin again. Instead, after some experimentation, they settled on mirrors: People could spend time checking out their profile, fixing their hair, examining their teeth. Again, problem solved—no more complaints.

Another: There's a reason you have to walk through a maze of velvet ropes to get to the teller at some banks. Someone discovered that by dividing a space into smaller measurable segments, our minds tell us that the wait is shorter. We mentally break up our wait into manageable chunks. We're less reminded of how long our wait is than when we see a long uninterrupted straight line down the street.

These are fairly simple tricks of perception, and you the customer are fooled by them (and other techniques like them) on a daily basis. Best of all? Tactics that free us from waiting in a visible line at all.

Consider this one of the benefits of living in a consumer-driven economy: In the thirty or so years since David Maister and Dr. Queue published their findings, companies have taken the hint. It's a brave new world of waiting out there, folks. New technologies are coming out every day to help measure, alleviate, streamline, and if possible eradicate the phenomenon of the physical queue. Some decades ago, some genius introduced the world to the take-a-number ticket dispenser. "Queue management" companies with names like Emerge Queue, Nemo-Q, QLess, Q-nomy, Q-net, Q-matic (I could go on) offer solutions that not only promise greater efficiency for the companies that use their products, but also offer the illusion that there isn't even a line. A customer often feels less trapped when there's no visible social structure to feel trapped in.

People-counting sensors, coupled with predictive algorithms, help stores know how many people will be rushing to check out at the same time. There are self-service kiosks at the movie theater, in airports, in casinos. At the university bookstore, a smartphone app keeps a student actively informed about his place in line, while he continues to browse the book rack. When it's his turn, he gets a Short Message Service (SMS) message. If he's a no-show, the system quickly sends the same message to the next person in the virtual line. And who doesn't simply pay their bills online anymore? One day we might look back at the queue and determine that it was a particularly twentieth-century phenomenon. Someone could write a song: "Where Have All the Line-Standers Gone?"

The illusion that we are trapped in line is increasingly being replaced by the illusion that we aren't. Technically, people are in line as much as they ever were, but the lines are becoming invisible, virtual. There may be as many slips and skips as there ever were, but because we can't see them, who's going to complain? Fix the perception, fix the problem. Sometimes there are life-and-death situations, or issues of social injustice, in which the invisibility of the line can lead to real problems (the so-called VA scandal that hounded the Obama administration in 2014 is a good example of that). But for the most part? As far as I'm concerned, if the problem really is all in my mind, that's good enough.

There may never be a physical line-standing robot brought to market, but make no mistake: Machines are taking over the act of line standing. Xavier, my savior! In this one area of life, at least, I welcome the coming robot takeover.

Bored (Video) Games

WAITING IN LINE 3D

The premise of Waiting in Line 3D couldn't be simpler: You are a man standing in an unmoving line, forced to punch yourself to stay awake. The game—which can be played for free online—is designed to resemble the game Wolfenstein 3D, pixelated in 1990s fashion, with a hypnotic soundtrack to match. Unlike Wolfenstein 3D, which has its protagonist running through castles shooting hordes of cartoonish Nazi villains, here you can only jump—OK, more like hop—and swivel around to see all the people in line behind you, or (by pressing the space bar) punch yourself in the face. You have a health bar that shows both your health (or lack thereof) and how awake you are. If you don't punch yourself in the face, you fall asleep (and therefore lose). If you punch yourself too much in the face, you die (and therefore lose).

The game is a lesson in fatalism. You fall asleep at a quicker rate than your body heals after you punch yourself. In other words, eventually you will always lose. It's a neat idea that—appropriate to its subject matter—is fun for about a minute, ideally designed for the masochists among us. And that's as the creator of the game, Rajeev Basu, wanted it: "So the game isn't interesting, exciting, or fun," he said, "I think we succeeded." I agree.

PAPERS, PLEASE!

Papers, Please!—created by Lucas Pope—focuses less on the drudgery of the line stander and more on the drudgery of the person serving the line standers. The year is 1982. You play an immigration inspector at a border station between two fictional Eastern European dictatorships—Arstotzka and Kolechia, each as grim as the other—that are at war with each other. The game has an appropriately Iron Curtain aesthetic in its gameplay, its visual style, and its music.

Day in and day out, you process passports and paperwork as people pass by your desk. You decide whom to green-stamp and whom to red-stamp (and whom to lock up, in the case of spies, smugglers, terrorists, or war criminals), based on whether they have the correct paperwork (and whether that paperwork is genuine or not). You work to keep your family fed and healthy; the more people you process the more you're paid (which is barely enough to live on), which you can augment sometimes by accepting bribes. If you make a mistake—by letting a person with the wrong paperwork into the country, for instance—you are fined. Things are so tense between Arstotzka and Kolechia by the end of the month that you are given the power to summarily execute line standers if you perceive in them a threat.

While the gameplay reflects the drudgery of its subject matter in its plodding, hypnotic quality, Papers, Please! is significantly more engaging than Waiting in Line 3D, even (dare I say it?) sometimes kinda fun. For one thing, it has a variety of possible story lines slipped in here or there amid the processing of endless line standers, as the work gradually begins to take an emotional toll on the immigration officer.

There are a variety of ways the game can end, nearly all of them bleak. Depending on the decisions you make, the poor immigration officer can go broke; he can be arrested and sentenced to hard labor; he can be put to death for failing his duties; his entire family can die of sickness; or he can flee to a neighboring country to avoid persecution (sometimes while leaving family members to face the wrath of the regime). And so forth.

The best that can be hoped for is nearly completely succeeding in his duties, including turning back terrorist attacks. In that case, the checkpoint remains open and you keep your bleak little job. This unlocks the game's endless mode, so that you can continue to process paperwork for ever and ever, without end. So hurray, I guess?

THE ARTIST IS PRESENT
The video game The Artist Is Present is based on the performance art piece of the same name (which it also shares with the subsequent HBO documentary about the event) by Marina Abramović, on the occasion of a retrospective of her work. Held at the Museum of

Modern Art (MoMA) in New York City, the piece consisted of Marina sitting in a chair for hours each day the museum was open, while thousands of visitors took turns sitting in the chair opposite her. Marina would spend a moment composing herself before each visitor, before making eye contact, opening herself to the visitor. For many, it was a highly emotional experience—the documentary shows many people spontaneously shedding a tear or two—as Marina and her guest silently shared a "presence." All told, Marina sat in that chair for 736½ grueling hours over the course of three months.

The piece received remarkable buzz—no doubt helped by the attendance of people like James Franco and Lady Gaga—and pretty quickly became a story in its own right due to the length of the lines. It didn't help that once someone sat down with Marina, the guest could hold her attention for as long as he liked. People would wait all day, only to be turned away when the museum closed at night. They began camping out at night in front of the MoMA and instituting unofficial numbering systems. For some, the wait to see her was itself part of the experience. The experience of time—slowed down almost to the point of stopping—became part of the artistic subject under investigation. Marina herself, at the beginning of each day, would write the number of hours and days on the wall of the exhibit. The experience of empty time the line stander might feel mirrors the experience of the artist herself.

So appropriately enough, the video game based on the performance art—created by Pippin Barr, found online for free—is as much about the wait as it is about Abramović. The screen is made to look like an old Atari 8-bit side-scroller with all those sharp, blocky pixelated edges. The avatar enters MoMA—if it's open, as the video-game museum keeps to the same hours the actual museum does. If the real museum is closed, you'll be told you can't enter. Once inside, your avatar buys a ticket and then joins the long line to see Marina. People get in line behind you. And then you just wait. And wait. And wait. All you see for 95 percent of your time in the game is people standing in single file with paintings in the background.

The line moves slowly. When I played, I wondered at first whether the line moved at all. But it does. The player might be forgiven for opening another window on their browser, to find something else to do while the line slowly dwindles. I can't say how long my avatar spent in line—several hours, I want to say, but the wait time can change each time you play. But eventually you do make it to Marina. Your reward for waiting it out? Seeing Marina, rendered Atari-style, in close up, for as long as you like.

I love the concept, but I doubt people playing will feel the same "presence"—nor the eagerness to share that presence—with a computer as they would with Marina in person. But as a virtual representation of what it feels like to wait in line, I don't think the game can be beat. It's definitely the most boring and the most grueling of all three games mentioned here, and I doubt that anyone would want to play it twice. I therefore declare it the winner.

CHAPTER FOUR

QUEUETOPIA
The Body Politic Waits Its Turn

What makes the queue such a potent political symbol in a modern democracy? In 1950, Winston Churchill—out of office since 1945, but seeking to return to parliament—delivered a speech that spoke directly to a daily frustration of countless British housewives (who bore the brunt of daily shopping) in the postwar years. He was attacking the policies of his political rivals of the British Labour Party, whom he derided as socialists and equated with the Communists of the Soviet Union. Churchill claimed that Labour's policies were not leading Britain to the utopia socialism promised, but to the queue becoming a "permanent, continuous feature of our life," as the government continued to play a larger and larger role in Brits' daily lives.

Churchill coined a word for this occasion: *queuetopia*. Here was the true direction Britain was headed under socialism, not utopia. Counter to the socialists, Churchill proposed freer markets, where competition would keep prices affordable, customers content, citizens self-reliant, and the size and role of government reasonably contained. Though rarely used anymore, the punning neologism— and the sentiment behind it—stuck, eventually entering the *Oxford English Dictionary*. And voters must have agreed: They voted Churchill back into office the following year. So much for the myth of the patient British queuer.

And so began the ongoing vilification of the queue that continues to this day on both sides of the Atlantic. I think this practice should be called queue-baiting, like "Red-baiting." As news began to filter out from behind the Iron Curtain about the long lines there, the queue became associated with Communism, or socialist-leaning policies in general.

For instance, in 1979, Maggie Thatcher borrowed from Churchill's playbook to vault herself into political office: Her famous poster carried the words LABOUR ISN'T WORKING in large letters—a clever slogan, pointing at once to Britain's high unemployment rate and to the failures of the Labour Party—displayed a (heavily manipulated) photograph of one endless "dole queue," people waiting to receive unemployment checks. Thirty years later in the United States, Mitt Romney's campaign—with some minimal changes in coloring—used the exact same poster but changed the slogan to Obama Isn't Working (not quite so zingy as Thatcher's).

Meanwhile, attempts to nationalize or simply regulate industry meet the same rhetorical appeal to citizen's wait times. Vote the Conservative ticket if you don't want to see long lines down every block and every citizen indentured to the red tape of government. Want a shorter wait? Deregulate. Privatize. While most prominent during the Cold War, queue-baiting remains an often-used tool: The predicted increased wait to see your doctor was the first weapon conservative pundits drew in the attempt to turn back the tide of Obamacare.

Queue-baiting taps into the popular fear that we have become—are becoming ever more—Machine-Made Man, automatons trapped in the cogs of a technocratic nanny state. To stand in line in order to be served by others violates our notion of the self-made individual. The promise to turn back Queuetopia is the promise to revert us to our "natural" state before automation, before state bureaucracy, before consumer culture. And while there may be a bit of truth in this formulation of what the line represents,

The Patriotic Queue

Our feelings about line standing change along with the political mood. For instance, in times of high patriotism—such as during wars with wide support—the queue might be seen as the embodiment of a collective, in which everyone should be treated equally and fairly. It reflects a spirit of "we're all in this together." As the French peasants reminded themselves, "Patriotism stands in queue," steeling themselves to wait. (And wait. And wait.) The tedium is temporary; the war will one day end. Do your part. Get in line. Buy war bonds. Get your flu shots. Not long ago, I heard the historian Jean Ashton on NPR offhandedly characterize the 1950s as a time when Americans "stood in line."

"People had just gone through World War Two," she explained. "They were used to trusting the government. And they were used to being obedient. Some historians say the whole of the Second World War entailed people standing in line." (Her implication being that we are much less willing to do so today.)

That same eagerness to get in line might be seen, by someone critical of patriotic fervor, as an example of conformity, anti-intellectualism, mindless fealty to authority. Such a critic might see the people in line as sheep, as consumers blindly following the actions and tastes of others.

Such was the view of the left-wing German social

critic Walter Benjamin, for instance, who complained that "the mob, impelled by a frenetic hatred of the life of the mind, has found a sure way to annihilate it in the counting of heads. Given the slightest opportunity, they form ranks and advance into artillery barrages and department stores in marching order. No one sees further than the back before him, and each is proud to be thus exemplary for the eyes behind."

Benjamin, a Jewish intellectual writing in a Germany that was ramping up for war—an atmosphere hostile to both Jews and intellectuals—might have had good reason to find this impulse to order troublesome.

---

it tends to obscure what's really causing the delay, as well as our motivations for standing in line.

Take Churchill's England, for instance. There is some irony in the fact that Churchill blames socialism for problems that were visible at least as early as 1942, when he himself was prime minister. In truth, far from representing a socialist Queuetopia, the long lines in England's particular case represented a corporate one (we might remember that businesses are bureaucracies, too, as anyone who has ever tried to personally contact the president of a large corporation will find out). So what was the cause of the mess?

HOTBEDS OF DISCONTENT

England, circa 1942: the year that government officials first acknowledged that queueing was a problem. World War II raged on. The Blitz had turned London into rubble. British forces were spread out far and wide over Europe and the Pacific. A stunning number of British citizens—men and women—had been mobilized in one capacity or another to support the war effort. And as women—housewives, mothers—entered the factories, they quickly discovered the foremost limitation of the modern workday: There's never a hell of a lot time left over when it's done. When did they have time to do their grocery shopping, when they were busy working all the damn time for the war effort?

This meant schlepping down to the shops during the lunch hour or after work—no rest for the weary—when every other woman in the city happened to be doing her shopping as well. It was a daily sight in wartime London: long lines of women stretched outside London shops with their baskets and handbags. You can bet there would be a long wait. When surveyed, nearly a third of working women listed "shopping difficulties" as their primary complaint about working.

The other problem was with the retailers who sold to them. For one thing, grocery stores didn't operate the way they do now: large modern self-service stores, shelves brimming with products, open early in the morning and late into the night. Instead, shops were more limited—the butcher, the baker, the candlestick maker, with a separate line for each out the door—and every product was delivered to the service counter by the clerk. These stores also had limited hours and limited staff, who kept hours roughly concurrent to the hours of the factory, including a break at lunchtime (made unavoidable by law, the Shops Act of 1912). The woman worker might clock out at 5:00 p.m., and the shop workers would clock out at 6:00, leaving the smallest of windows to get shopping done.

There was political pressure for shop owners to keep their doors open until eight or nine p.m. to accommodate workers, but retailers pushed back against this suggestion with strong lobbying: This would impinge on their freedom as citizens, they argued. In truth, they were resistant to implementing any changes that might cost them money. The fewer hours one is open, the less one has to pay employees for those hours. With so many people employed in the war effort, able-bodied workers were scarce and hence more expensive. And because resources during the war were already stretched so thin, they knew they would sell all the products on their shelves no matter how few hours they were open.

In nearly all matters, the Ministry of Food steadfastly supported the rights of business owners, ideologically committed to the invisible hand of the market. This is not to say its members did nothing about the problems faced by women: They reluctantly imposed a complicated system of rationing. This did nothing to reduce the lines, but it did mean that the women at the front of the line couldn't buy out all the products before those at the back got their turn. Though rationing proved to be extremely popular—91 percent of women polled approved of these measures—retailers and the Ministry of Food grumbled that it was (as an internal memo put it) "a restriction of personal liberty."

There were also complaints from the industries these women were employed in. Oftentimes women simply had to take time off work to go shopping; they could be away for hours, standing in line. Some women's time was considered more valuable to the war effort than others, leading to experimental schemes that gave priority service to some (munitions factory workers, for instance), which led to popular resentment against these ladies who got to skip the wait. They were accused of being "cheeky" when they walked to the head of the line, and ordered all the best cuts of meat. The experiment was dropped after too many complaints.

No one was happy, least of all women. Vocal complaints grew louder and louder, to the point where some feared revolt in the streets. "Hotbeds of discontent" is how one Ministry of Food official characterized the queues, in a widely circulated 1942 memo. Something would have to be done. For evidence, he cited a German authority on the question (an odd choice considering whom England was at war with at the time):

The queue is an ugly creature and a breeder of rumors. As the latter it is a political problem; there is no place for rumor in wartime. During a war people's energies can be put to better use than stirring up trouble by spreading rumors. . . . Where there is a queue people imagine there is a scarcity; where scarcity is presumed irrational appetite arises. Scarcity causes more queues, queues increase the urge to get 'just one more.' . . . There has, in fact, developed the professional queuer, a malignant and odious breed.

Rather than looking at the structural problems that were causing delays, the authorities opted to put the line stander in the same category as people who make runs on banks, hoard gasoline during crises, and empty food shelves before an impending hurricane. (A fairly common tactic: Note how the peasants of the French Revolution are always characterized as a mob, as opposed to, say, concerned citizens engaged in a collective action.) They were helped by a fact that everyone knew—that women are irrational creatures, driven by herd psychology. Women were being whipped up into a frenzy of fear that supplies wouldn't last.

Men pretended to scratch their heads quizzically, to ponder the impenetrable divide that separates masculine brain from feminine brain. Why did they subject themselves to standing in line? You don't ever see men standing in line! Was there something embedded in the female psychology that drove women to queue? Perhaps they even enjoy standing in line!

Might this irrational hysteria prove dangerous? Germany under the National Socialist Party was known to closely police the queues that formed there for subversive elements, and to employ "queue-taming" tactics, such as refusing to serve queuers or simply keeping a heavy police presence at hand on days when long lines could be expected. For a time, the Ministry of Food, in conversation with retailers, seriously considered some of these methods, before quietly shelving them as being too, well . . . Nazi.

But really the whole discussion was a feint. By claiming that the protesters were too irrational, authorities pretended that nothing could be done—at least not without violating the holy tenets of capitalism by impinging on the freedom of business owners. Once the Ministry of Food took the position that women had created the mess—a clear-cut case of blaming the victim—the logical next step was to make women responsible for cleaning it up. Having convinced themselves there was nothing they could do, officials washed their hands of the entire matter.

On the British Love of Queueing

At least one person found the situation in England comical. The humorist George Mikes, a Hungarian emigrant to England, poked gentle fun at English customs—including their predilection to form queues—in his 1946 book *How to Be an Alien:*

> *In England, people do not often get excited. They do not enjoy many things but they love to queue.*
>
> *In Europe, if people are waiting at a bus-stop they look bored and half asleep. When the bus arrives they fight to get on it. Most of them leave on the bus and some are very lucky and leave in an ambulance. One Englishman waits at a bus-stop and, even if there are no other people there, he starts a queue.*

This state of affairs continued for roughly a decade. Women resorted to a patchwork of tactics (asking neighbors to pitch in, forming cooperative neighbors' shopping leagues, taking time off work). What else could they do? When the British government considered the question of whom the government was to serve first, women were at the back of the line. Women were politically powerless, in all but having the right to vote. All that was needed, then,

> The biggest and best queues are in front of cinemas. These queues have large cards that say: Queue here for 4s 6d; Queue here for 9s 3d; Queue here for 16s 8d. Nobody goes to a cinema if it does not have cards telling customers to queue.
>
> At weekends, an Englishman queues up at the bus-stop, travels out to Richmond, queues up for a boat, then queues up for tea, then queues up for ice cream, then queues up some more because it is fun, then queues up at the bus-stop when he wants to go home. He has a very good time.
>
> Many English families spend pleasant evenings at home just by queueing for a few hours. The parents are very sad when the children leave them and queue up to go to bed.

was a charismatic politician with wiles enough to tap into their discontent.

THE POWER TO MAKE OTHERS WAIT

It's always the case: One person's utopia will be another person's dystopia. The system that privileges one class of people will disadvantage another. At issue: How do we determine how to fairly allocate goods and services in a society? Whose freedom is privileged? In England, the cost of such freedom came at the cost of women, whose lack of any such freedom dictated when they could and could not shop.

Similarly, when conservatives decry that under Obamacare people will have to wait longer to see their doctor, they are ignoring the fact that wait times don't get much longer in the U.S. than in hospital emergency rooms, full of the uninsured. They also ignore that private corporations are bureaucracies, too, only calibrated to serve some more quickly than others. To the person in pain, hours into her wait at the hospital, perhaps a genuine Queuetopia—in which wait times are shared equally by all—might not sound so bad.

Just who is in line? Who isn't? From a wide-enough lens, such questions turn out to have broad political implications. When Thomas Carlyle turned his attention across the English Channel toward France's revolution, he saw few rich men waiting their turns in the breadlines. The line has traditionally been the domain of the poor, and particularly poor women (as Walter Benjamin noted, "the parade-march of penury, standing in line, is the invention of women"). In America, you might add race to the mix of class and gender inequality. The lower down the pecking order you are, the more you will find yourself in line. Inversely, we might define the powerful as "those who do not wait." Dr. Queue's notion of slips and skips can be applied at the societal level: The rich slip, the poor get skipped.

Power and waiting are inversely linked in human society. So argues sociologist Barry Schwarz, who began his career studying the linkages between power structures and the ways we wait. Everywhere you look, at all levels, you see microtransactions of power being played out, according to who has power over whose time. Time is money and money is power, and every day we buy and spend all three. To Schwarz, time has exchange value; it's a currency not unlike money.

It's not difficult to see how the rich exchange money for time. More expensive grocery stores mean fewer crowds and more cashiers. They can go through an agent—for a fee—to get tickets to sports venues or concert halls, rather

The American Way

The photograph is iconic; you've doubtlessly seen it. A long line of African Americans packed tightly together stretches across the lower third of the frame, men, women, and children looking reasonably well dressed in long coats and brimmed 1930s-style headwear, standing erect and miserable, appearing weary on their feet. One woman hangs a wicker basket in the crook of her elbow. A man carries a burlap sack. A couple more hold silvery tin pails, the kind that miners used to carry their lunches in. No one smiles. The line does not appear to be going anywhere anytime soon. What could they be waiting for? For bread? For work? Nothing frivolous, that's for sure.

They stand in front of a painted billboard backdrop that takes up over half the frame. On it we see the very image of white middle-class mobility. There, the classic nuclear American family (father, mother, son, daughter, and dog) look ridiculously happy to be driving nowhere in particular in a shiny automobile. They aren't stuck in line. They're moving down the highway at breakneck speed, wind in their hair, waiting for no one because they don't have to. The billboard reads: WORLD'S HIGHEST STANDARD OF LIVING, followed by, "There's no way like the American Way." The irony is rich. The photograph suggests that there are two separate (and unequal) American Ways. One moves. The other stands still.

The photograph is somewhat deceptive and has often been used out of context. On the surface, it appears to comment on the fact that economic failures hurt some groups of Americans harder than others. Yet in reality, the photograph was taken in the aftermath of the Great Ohio River Flood of 1937. The photograph was part of a set published in *Life* magazine by ace photographer Margaret Bourke-White. The other photos are what you'd expect. Water, water everywhere. Beauty in destruction. Worried faces. A flooded racetrack. Submerged automobiles. Things used as boats that were not originally intended to be boats. And so forth. So the American Way photograph was not evidence of systemic racism as such; these were people simply waiting for emergency supplies.

Does the deception matter? The photograph is such an elegant encapsulation of real problems, that I'm inclined to forgive those who have used it out of context. The photograph at the very least might serve as a useful reminder from time to time. Such is often the way with famous photographs: Stripping them of their context makes them all the more powerful. They become iconic, universal, timeless. Floods come and go, but it seems that the queue—as Jesus said of the poor—will always be with us.

than wait out in the cold with the common folk. Their well-paid doctors serve fewer clients; sometimes they even make house calls. Their first-class tickets allow them a priority lane through security screening to be the first ones to board the plane. Even when they do have to wait, they do so in better accommodations—the VIP Lounge at the airport, say, separate from the rank and file.

Their time is more valuable than our time, the message goes. I remember when it was popular to calculate how much money Bill Gates would have to find in the street to make it worthwhile for him to spend three seconds to pick it up (answer: a helluva lot). The implication is that Bill Gates can't be bothered to wait for anyone. What this means is that nearly everyone must instead wait for Bill Gates. Seeking an audience? Get in line. If he agrees to see you at all, then you must bend your schedule to accommodate his, waiting hat in hand. (Though arguably many of us wait on Bill every day by being forced to use Windows.)

The more power or money you have, the more influence you have on others' time. To get the ear of your boss, make an appointment. Show up early; never be late. You make your schedule fit his, because his time is more expensive than yours. We see the patterns of dominance and submission throughout society: When you wait, you are submitting yourself to the dominance of others. Meanwhile, your boss has far more latitude: He can make meetings run long, prioritize a phone call while you just sit there awkwardly waiting, and show up at your office cubicle unannounced.

The dominant person might even use his power to make you wait as a cudgel, as a retaliatory weapon. Schwarz cites a story about how President Harry Truman once made Winthrop Aldrich, the Chase Manhattan Bank president, wait outside the Oval Office for thirty minutes. "When I was a United States senator and headed the war investigation committee," Truman reportedly explained to a staff member, "I had to go to New York to see this fella Aldrich. Even though I had an appointment he had me cool my heels for an hour and a half. So just relax. He's got a little while to go yet." And if you think using this power is limited to President Truman, see the example of New Jersey governor Chris Christie in the "Bridge-Gate Scandal" of 2013, when Christie appointees allegedly shut down lanes of the George Washington Bridge as retaliation against political rivals, inconveniencing thousands.

Sometimes the less powerful among us get to use this weapon too, like the poorly paid restaurant waiter using deliberate and diffident slowness when serving you. Waiting tables is a job that, as the name says, literally requires the worker to wait and thereby submit to customers. That clerk, Schwarz suggests, is simply reclaiming some of the power that was lost to her by dint of her job. And as frustrating as poor service might be from the standpoint of the customer, we might sometimes remember to be sympathetic.

At all stages of life, we are taught to equate waiting with punishment. Enforced delay establishes (or reestablishes) the power of the person who can control another person's time. The naughty child is put into *time-out*. Misbehaving students are put into *detention*, measured by empty time.

Line Standing as Ceremony

People sometimes want to submit to others, of course. The starstruck fan who lines up for a photograph with the celebrity she admires. The congregants who line up to shake hands with the newly minted bride and groom. In 1999, when George Lucas released *The Phantom Menace,* the first new Star Wars film in sixteen years, fans camped out for weeks outside cineplexes all over the country. At funerals we get in line to "pay our respects." Line standing is one way we voluntarily show deference, especially if we greatly admire the person. Schwarz gives the example of John F. Kennedy's funeral at the Capitol Rotunda, in which a quarter of a million people lined up for nearly ten hours in miserable weather to pay their respects. Most recently this happened at Nelson Mandela's funeral, with thousands waiting in serpentine lines, including some of the most powerful people on earth, a voluntary and symbolic act of submission toward the late great man.

American prisoners are said to be *doing time*, and if that punishment weren't already enough, American prisons are notorious for the amount of time a prisoner will spend standing in line every single day (at the chow hall, at the canteen, to see the doctor . . .). At all moments, inmates are reminded of how powerless they truly are and how powerful the institution is that controls their time.

There is an entire macrocosm of waiting, measured in seconds, minutes, hours, days, years, in minuscule and not-so-minuscule, invisible and visible, gestures of submission and domination. What gets decided is who gets first dibs at acquiring the things that a society produces. First come, first served? Perhaps at the local level, among people of more-or-less equal standing. Too often, however, the powerful get first dibs over the weak, the rich over the poor, men over women, whites over blacks, white-collars over blue-collars, and Americans over the rest of the world.

We see the difference most starkly on election day, as news filters out about how long the urban residents of politically contentious states (Ohio, Pennsylvania, Florida) have to wait at the ballot box, up to eight hours in some cases. On a daily basis, the urban poor (many of them minorities) already wait longer than any other group in America, both because of a lack of affluence and because of population density. Anyone who can afford to moves to where there is more of everything relative to the individual (grocery stores, doctors, teachers, lanes of highway).

Ideally, election day is the day when all citizens are equal. Ideally, each person's vote is of entirely the same worth. But the cost is vastly different, depending where you live. If waiting really is currency, as Barry Schwarz contends, how can we fail to agree with critics (such as Rachel Maddow) who have argued that these long lines are a modern form of poll tax?

Perhaps it's unfortunate that there's no Queuetopia Party to vote for. At least in urban areas of Ohio and Pennsylvania, they might do pretty well.

INSIDE THE LINE

We've seen a temptation, from those looking from outside the line, to characterize the line stander as somehow emptied of thoughts and feelings, powerless, obedient, submissive, herdlike (Machine-Made Man, in other words). This, we're told, is the danger of Queuetopia. As someone who has stood in quite a few lines myself, I believe there's some truth in this. But it also ignores all the microtransactions of submission and domination that often occur *within* the line, as well. After all, people don't simply empty their heads as soon as they queue up.

The act of stepping into line is like putting a stake in the ground: submissive to the people in front of you, dominant

Americans First

Americans in particular, it seems, are driven by an ideology of "first dibs." Perhaps the importance of the line in our political imagination has to do with being a colonized country, in which the first to plant a flag in "virgin" territory determines who owns the property. "We were here first," anti-immigration protesters loudly declaim. Meanwhile, illegal immigrants are accused of "cutting in line" in front of decent, law-abiding immigrants waiting their turn (and in front of white Americans, afraid that darker-skinned people will poach their territory). The anti-immigration crowd of course ignores that, for the groups they are targeting (Mexicans, South Americans) there is not even a line for them to get in: The U.S. government puts severe limitations on the type of person who can even be considered for immigration. And they forget, too, that we are at our essence a nation of line cutters: Native Americans might remind us who really was here first.

to the people behind you. Especially when lines are extremely long, all sorts of considerations have to be made to protect that stake. What happens, for instance, when the delay exceeds the ability of the human body to stand in line that long? What happens when the wait takes a day, a week, a month? In that time, people need to eat, sleep, take a leak, check their email inbox. Then line standing is not so simple. You might negotiate with the guy behind you to step out for a bite to eat, but how long is it fair for the guy to protect your stake? But can the person who leaves to go drink in a bar for three hours simply return to his spot when he's done? Would that be fair?

Unfortunately, there are no rules for fairness set in stone. They must be negotiated each time, and these negotiations can be complex. What do such negotiations look like? Two studies shed light on the subject, one by Leon Mann, who studied the lines of soccer fans that would form overnight for playoff matches, the other by F. Neil Brady, who studied the lines of Star Wars fans camping out for tickets to *The Phantom Menace* throughout the U.S. Both studies reveal that lines reflect a social system in miniature, full of competition, political alliances, in-groups and out-groups, and positions of power, according to the principle of first come, first served. Machine-made men? Hardly!

For instance, both men observed the tendency of queuers at the front of the line to form cliques, groups with an established membership and social identity. They define themselves against late-comers, establishing theirs as the dominant position. This lets them create rules that govern behavior among their own members, allowing for people to leave the line if they need to. Leon Mann, for instance, noted shift systems, in which members of that clique allowed each other to take time off (with the understanding that the remaining members would protect their stake). Otherwise they might leave a marker ("a labeled box, folding chair, or sleeping bag") that they can return to, provided that they are not gone too long, after which it becomes socially acceptable for angry late-comers to chuck their markers and deny them reentry.

Brady discovered even more complex systems, perhaps accounted for by the extreme length of time many of these line standers waited—for a week or more! They made lists, they handed out numbers, they logged hours. Rules become formalized in sometimes strange ways. For instance, one such clique out of New Orleans established the first sixty spots as theirs, and determined each member's place within that sixty by the total number of hours each member waited, tallied up at the end. As long as the line stander was a member of that original group, he could take off as much time as he wanted. If he was content with the sixtieth spot, theoretically he didn't have to wait at all, leading to an absurd situation in which the sixty-first person in line likely waited much longer for his ticket than the sixtieth.

The farther back you are in the line, the less you feel a member of the collective identity of the line, standing farther away from the person in front of you. For one thing, you've had less time to become acquainted with those around you, and you have even less opportunity now that the people in front of you have had time to clique; by now, they have had their own conversations, understandings, and in-jokes that you are not privy to.

You also simply have less invested in the queue: You haven't sunk as much time into the thing. Especially for something as inconsequential as movie tickets, the cost of reneging is small. At the very end, the line splinters like the frays at the end of the rope. The person at the very back hesitates for a minute, deciding if he is or is not a member of the queue, whether the wait will be worth it: He, after all, has the option to just say "The hell with it!" and wait for the movie to be available for streaming.

What do these adaptations to the normal ethics of queueing reveal? The norm of first come, first served is a fairly decent organizing principle, all things considered, but it is almost never perfectly implemented and is far from being the only consideration to determine what's fair. As F. Neil Brady argues, FCFS is an ideal with ethical simplicity ("one enters at the rear and waits; to leave is to forfeit one's position"), but it is also an ideal that quickly breaks down in the face of lived experience. People talk to one another. They learn that their neighbors in line aren't faceless, soulless automatons. They cooperate with one another. They make allowances for one another.

It is an unrealized ideal, too, because of the ambiguous identity of the line. No two lines operate in the same way. The line to wait for movie tickets operates on a different principle than the line to see Nelson Mandela interred, than the one to see your doctor in the waiting room, than the conga line. We use the same word to describe different

---

What did seem to take over was interpersonal association and group cooperation. People waited in line, but they had fun while they waited; and they formed "communities." They shared interests, they played games, they prepared food, they told stories, they did favors for each other, they fought, they resolved disputes, they sought leadership and conferred authority, they protected the community against intrusion, they adopted sanctions and norms, they reinforced values and ideals of the group, they made plans for the future, they discussed the deeper spiritual meanings of things, they had spiritual experiences. . . . In short, they lived a "mini-life" while waiting to buy tickets.

—F. NEIL BRADY,
"LINING UP FOR STAR-WARS TICKETS"

---

sorts of activities, because all those things resemble one another. Out of this confusion comes the need to set terms, which will be different for each group of people.

Think of the many types of lines people have experience with: traffic lines, waiting for the light at the crosswalk, parking lots, restroom facilities, emergency rooms, organizational hierarchies and deference to authorities ("line of authority or command"), lines of reasoning, a line in a marching band, football offensive lines, ordering hamburgers at a fast food drive-up window, land rush lines, taking seats in an airplane, door crasher sales at department stores, automobile registration lines, electronic buzzers at restaurants. Some of these "lines" have sequence, some do not; some have waiting, some do not; some have a starting time, some do not; some have a variable price, others a fixed price; some have many servers, some have one or none; some allow for representation, some do not. It is no wonder that people might confuse one experience with another and exhibit the kinds of confusion and mental conflict that this study has observed.

—F. NEIL BRADY,
"LINING UP FOR STAR-WARS TICKETS"

One might interpret this ambiguity pessimistically or optimistically. It is either a failure to live up to the lofty principle of FCFS or an opportunity to set up new agreements each time.

THE FUTURE OF THE QUEUE

Now that we seem to have successfully turned back the forces of Queuetopia in favor of the free market, what will the future of waiting look like? Increasingly, it will be a thing that can be bought and sold, like any other commodity.

- We already see this trend in our airports, where a number of different services let elite customers pay to skip the line. First-class passengers have long gotten their own lines through security checkpoints, and now passengers can pay about $85 to skip the wait using Pre-Check. Even private companies have started getting into the racket. At least nine airports nationwide have contracts with CLEAR, a company that allows you to "breeze past the long lines and go straight to screening," for $179 a year.

- Theme parks, long known for their tremendously long lines, have found that they could capitalize on the commodification of waiting. Six Flags, Universal Studios, and Cedar Point all reflect the trend. Besides VIP tours, which cost anywhere from $250 (Six Flags) to $450 (Cedar Point) per person and guarantee access to the front of the line, they offer any number of intermediary passes, including Universal Express and Universal Express Unlimited, Fast Lane and Fast Lane Plus, and Flash Passes in Regular, Gold, and Platinum varieties (depending on whether you want your wait time reduced by 50 percent or 90 percent). The exception to this trend is Disney, whose FastPass is part of the basic package.

- Casinos—so-called theme parks for adults, such as Caesar's—have begun implementing priority lines for gamblers of a certain tier, who can bypass the wait at hotel check-in, at the buffet, at Starbucks, pretty much anywhere lines are known to form. While there is no way to expressly buy a pass, you could argue that you pay for the privilege by how much money you've lost gambling.

- Even cities have gotten into the business, implementing "high-occupancy toll lanes," otherwise known as Lexus lanes—letting people pay to use the car-pool lanes during rush hour. In Minneapolis, for instance, where I live, electronic billboards announce the cost of using these lanes, which changes throughout the morning and afternoon commute, based on traffic flow.

And so forth: an ever-growing structure of slips and skips, it seems, based on affluence. The question is: Should it be so? For one thing, it seems to me that many of these companies are capitalizing on their own shitty service. What's the incentive to improve service, when they're making even more money because of it? Why not make service worse, so that more people are driven to buy their Flash Pass? (This is essentially what they are doing: After all, when people cut in front of you, they make your wait that much longer.) Why change, when it all comes out as profit in the end?

Moreover, these schemes corrupt a civic ideal and normalize that corruption. This is the argument Harvard-based political philosopher Michael Sandel makes in his recent book *What Money Can't Buy*, which inventories all the many things money is buying but, he believes, shouldn't be. There are things that should be held sacred, not up for sale. Paying to cut in line joins a list of things now bought and sold that once were not: luxury jail cells for the rich, permits to hunt endangered animals, autographs of baseball players. And while the rich have always found ways to get around the principle of first come, first served, he's dismayed by how thoroughly market logic is permeating once cherished ideals at all levels.

Sandel points to the proliferation of stories in recent years of people selling the service of standing in line. For instance, whenever there's a new Apple iPhone roll-out, there are stories of people either selling their spot in line to the highest bidder (reportedly for $2,500 in one instance!) or offering to wait in line for an hourly wage. Most of these are fairly informal arrangements, made by individuals over Craigslist.

But entrepreneurs, seeing a business opportunity, have gotten into the game as well. In New York City, for instance, there's SOLD Inc. (standing for Same Ole Line Dudes) offering both line-standing services to customers and line-management services to businesses: For $25 for the first hour, and $10 for subsequent hours, they'll wait for anything, including "Cronuts, an iPhone 6, the latest Air Jordans, or the hottest Bway tix in town." They even have special Cronut-delivery pricing: $65 per authentic pair from the Dominique Ansel Bakery on Spring Street.

But probably the epicenter of paid line standing is Washington, D.C., home of two prominent line-standing companies, Linestanding.com and Washington Express. There, paid stand-ins stand in single file in the halls of Congress and at the Supreme Court, many of them overnight, only to be replaced by highly paid lobbyists in expensive suits hours later. Often these line standers make it difficult for average members of the public—who can't really afford to pay $50 an hour to pay someone to wait—to get into these meetings, meaning they are attended mainly by those with the interests of business at heart.

Some have found this practice troubling, such as former congressman Barney Frank or Senator Claire McCaskill from Missouri, who in 2007 introduced an anti-line-standing bill as a "symbolic gesture" (meaning, of course, that she knew it would never be passed by Congress). "Once I realized this was happening, I was really offended," she told reporters. "This is the people's government and these should be the people's hearings. I have no problem with lobbyists getting into hearings, but they shouldn't be able to buy a seat."

Should people be able to pay to skip the line? Sandel thinks no. If you were to ask a free-market economist, however, the answer would be yes. According to market logic, paying for someone to stand in line for you corrects a pricing imbalance: If there are long lines outside of your establishment, you are obviously underpricing the goods you are offering.

If you raise the price to what the market can bear, you will reduce the lines. What paid line standers—ticket scalpers by another name—are doing is returning the price to what people are willing to pay, and profiting from the difference. Some people are willing to pay with their time, but there are some who would prefer to pay with their money. Ideally, instead of FCFS, every transaction between buyer and seller would resemble an auction, in which the highest bidder gets first dibs.

But there is something unsavory about a market logic that translates all questions of value into purely monetary terms. Sandel offers other examples as well: New York City's popular Shakespeare in the Park, for instance, which is meant to be a public service, free to all, but is swamped by people paid to buy up tickets. Campsites at popular national parks like Yosemite—costing a meager twenty dollars but in high demand—are being auctioned off on Craigslist. There were even scalpers selling tickets to see Pope Benedict XVI when he was here. Catholic leaders scolded: "You can't pay to celebrate a sacrament."

These are all things the market says are being drastically underpriced (sometimes as underpriced as something gets: free). But that's only if we accept that all things can and should be turned into commodities. Access to public hearings is supposed to be open to all, but in reality, they are likely to be attended only by those with money to spare. The Transportation Security Administration exists for the national security of all, but only those who can't afford otherwise are disadvantaged at the security check. Isn't there something kinda questionable about someone making a profit from what's supposed to be a public good, open to all?

In the age of the Internet and apps on our phones, I predict these trends will continue ever more quickly, spurred on by Silicon Valley free-market utopianism. Craigslist users will continue to offer their bodies as placeholders for a price. Sites like StubHub will continue to facilitate the resale of tickets, at a handsomely inflated price, for which someone, somewhere stood in line. Meanwhile, apps like MonkeyParking or ParkModo allow one driver to hold a parking space for another driver for a fee—out of which the company gets a commission—an act of renting out public space, and a violation of first come, first served.

Once upon a time, such transactions would have been considered seedy. Ticket scalping, illegal in some places, has never been more than warily accepted. Paying for access out of turn shares a kinship with a bribe. In any case, they come at the cost of those unwilling (and more important, unable) to pay for the service. As a civic ideal, first come, first served may never be fully realized. There will probably never be a perfect Queuetopia. But that doesn't mean we shouldn't try.

The Television Show About Nothing

Without a doubt, the television show that best captures the spirit of line standing—in all its contradictory and morally ambiguous splendor—would be *Seinfeld*, the show that purports to be "about nothing." Hardly an episode goes by in which someone isn't standing in line (waiting for a seat at the movies, a seat in the restaurant, or bread from the bakery). Fittingly, the show takes place in New York City, one of the most congested cities in the world, where everyone is in competition for limited resources. And what episodes don't feature Jerry, George, Elaine, or Kramer trying to wheedle their way to the front of any line worth standing in?

Arguably some of the show's pinnacle episodes are fully centered on the act of queueing. A characteristic one is "The Dinner Party," most of which takes place in a bakery line waiting for a chocolate babka that they are hoping to take to a dinner party. None of their desires is fully met (they receive a cinnamon babka instead of a chocolate one, and because they find a hair in it, they have to wait in line all over again). Needless to say, they never do get to the dinner party (a Kafka-approved ending). It is a show that privileges the process—usually a poorly designed one—over the outcome, and often that process involves the empty moments of standing in line. The pleasure of watching the show comes from hearing them bullshit and kvetch hilariously.

Because it does such a good job showing processes, *Seinfeld* has been used quite a few times to illustrate issues important to both operations researchers and to economists. For instance, economist Linda Ghent at Eastern Illinois University has compiled an impressive database of Seinfeld episodes coupled with the economic principles they illustrate, at the website The Economics of Seinfeld (with the wonderful web address, "Yadayadayadaecon.com").

For instance, the entire episode of "The Chinese Restaurant" takes place while Jerry, Elaine, and George wait for a table at a restaurant that's booked up, and which they've failed to make a reservation for. They first beg, and then finally try to bribe their way to a table, an example of both an "opportunity cost" (the trio agrees that it's worth $20 to them to forgo the wait) and a "rationing mechanism" (by bribing the host, they would behave as in a black market, which develops as a response to the rationing of goods, in this case a table in a restaurant). The attempt fails, forcing them to wait longer, while watching others who have arrived after them (who have made reservations) get their tables first (an example of slips and skips).

Over the course of the wait, Elaine even comes to question the fairness of the first come, first served rationing mechanism central to our understanding of justice. "It's not fair that people are served based on first come, first served," she complains. "It should be based on who's hungriest." There are certainly political philosophers out there who wouldn't disagree with her about that. As in "The Dinner Party," they never reach their destination; they finally walk out (or renege, in economics terminology). Tragically, the host calls them to their table a second too late.

But my favorite example is probably "The Soup Nazi," in which all the characters must individually weigh the high cost of getting the soup (i.e., a long line with strictly enforced rules), the large reward associated with that cost (i.e., soup that "will make your knees buckle"), and the gamble that you will not be served at all even after the long wait, due to the capricious nature of the so-called Soup Nazi. "No soup for you!," he loudly declares, if someone fails to meet his high expectations. He also has the power to charge customers different prices if they don't follow his rules (he charges George $2 for the bread that everyone else gets free, for daring to question him).

The Soup Nazi's business thrives because he basically has a monopoly: His soup is so good that people will forgo other soup and timidly suffer the long wait to eat at his establishment. The Soup Nazi can be capricious because he has no direct competitors and high consumer demand. That's why Elaine's revenge on him is so effective: When she gets ahold of his recipes, his market power is destroyed.

Strangely enough, the Soup Nazi was based on a

real individual, also in the soup business: Al Yeganeh, the "Soup Man" of New York City, who ran the Soup Kitchen International when *Seinfeld* was on the air. His restaurant was indeed renowned not just for the soup, but also for the long line down the block, and for his wrath when customers wouldn't follow the rules. Know what you want to order when you get to the counter. Be ready with your money. Speak quickly. Don't ask questions. Move to the extreme left after ordering. Yeganeh was known to sometimes reward compliance with these rules with free bread and fruit. Break these rules, and he would withhold bread and fruit, and (perhaps) soup.

Yeganeh didn't appreciate his portrayal on *Seinfeld*, saying that it ruined his life. Indeed, he has called Jerry Seinfeld "that clown" and once kicked Seinfeld out of his restaurant when he came in. ("No soup for you!" Yeganeh reportedly told Seinfeld, appropriately enough.) His rules—he certainly likes his rules—for speaking to the press now include "No use of the N word"—N as in Nazi. Yeganeh's concern for his portrayal seems a bit petty, especially if you consider how much money *Seinfeld* probably made him with the publicity.

But there is a case to be made on Yeganeh's behalf. However impersonal his rules and brusque his manner, they were designed to efficiently keep the line moving, especially important when there's a forty-five-minute wait around the block. Yeganeh believes that no transaction should last more than seven seconds, so have your money ready, know what you want to order, and then move your butt to make way for the next paying customer.

Through his brusqueness, he is teaching his customers queueing discipline in an unusually forward fashion. I imagine this is especially important to a buzzed-about place like his, a draw for tourists as much as for native New Yorkers, in which the general impulse is to hem and haw over what soup to order, to coo and gush, to ask whether this soup or that soup is vegan or gluten-free, and to take photos for your Instagram feed. Not at his establishment you don't!

So please, if you're at the front of the line, do as Jerry does in "The Soup Nazi" episode: Order quickly, quietly, and then get the hell out. Don't make a muck of it like Elaine or George. Those of us at the back of the line thank you.

CHAPTER FIVE

BILLIONS SERVED WORLDWIDE, ONE CHEESEBURGER AT A TIME

A Study in Cultural Contrasts

There's a video you can watch on YouTube, seemingly of a city park on a sunny day somewhere behind the Iron Curtain (the buildings, the vehicles, babushkas in head scarves, the washed-out grainy quality of the picture: They all have that stolid Soviet look to them). The Steadicam footage, obviously manned by someone on a motor vehicle, veers right approaching the park, where you see that a largish throng of people has gathered (a hundred maybe? . . . difficult to say). As the camera pans past them, you see that this throng is actually a queue, and extends around the corner of the park.

The soundtrack: a sprightly traditional Russian folk song, a wistful soprano, nimbly plucked guitar strings.

Surely this must be a love song, though an admittedly downbeat one. The lyrics, I imagine, tell of a woman separated from her lover by miles and years. As the song tempo increases at the chorus, so does the vehicle (10 miles per hour . . . 20 . . . faster . . .), and the people all meld into a mélange of drab 1980s-era clothing (that is, predominated by denim), whizzing by. The camera rounds yet another corner down an equally long block, and then another corner, and then still another, until what you thought would be hundreds of people is now clearly several thousand. And just what the hell are all these people waiting for anyway?

The video builds the viewer's anticipation. The camera rounds the final corner, and then slows to a stop, panning upward to reveal . . . a McDonald's sign?

FRONT-TO-BACK IN THE U.S.S.R.

A letdown, but I guess you had to be there. This McDonald's (as the YouTube description explains) was the first in the Soviet Union. The footage, then, would be from Moscow circa 1990, shortly after the market reforms enacted by Gorbachev. To believe some, this is what truly signaled the end of the Cold War. To heighten the symbolism, the restaurant was placed in Pushkin Square, the busiest in Moscow, not far from the Kremlin. The Soviet Union would collapse less than two years later.

A similar scene played out in Romania in 1995, a few years after the country's own revolution. I was twelve. I remember waking up uncomfortably early in the morning with my family to join the massive, festive crowd gathered in front of Bucharest's biggest department store, in Piaţa Unirii, Bucharest's central plaza. We stood in the shadow of a bright blimp-size blow-up Ronald McDonald doll tethered to the edge of the department store's roof. In direct line of sight in the distance, at the end of an imperious cobblestone boulevard lined with ornate faux Greco-Roman fountains, stood the unfinished palace of Romania's erstwhile dictator, Nicolae Ceauşescu. The palace was his grand shrine to himself (symbolizing nothing so much as his tyrannical waste and abuse), second in size only to the Pentagon as far as government buildings go. Ronald McDonald's permanent wave and smile seemed pointed in its direction: American triumphalism embodied. McDonald's marketing arm knows how to send a message.

In the decade following World War II, there had been a popular mantra among anti-Communist resistance movements in Romania: "The Americans are coming!" The hope was that American forces would invade Eastern Europe in the coming war with Russia and free them from Communist oppression. Now the Americans were here at last, decades late, in the form of a fast-food franchise. It's been reported that some were reciting this half-century-old mantra when McDonald's opened its doors.

Whatever McDonald's signified for your average Romanian following generations of dictatorship, for someone like my father (ever the capitalist queue-o-phobe), it signified American efficiency, motivated customer service, product reliability and consistency (they might peddle blah, mass-produced fast food, but at least no one worries that McDonald's might run out of Big Macs, or that their beef isn't really beef). The doors opened that morning, the scrum streamed in, organized themselves (with help from queue-minders directing traffic) into about twenty lines. These were served at a quick clip by about twenty cash registers.

"See this?" my father said in a low voice as we approached the counter. "I heard they had to send all of their employees abroad for training. This way they can be reprogrammed. You'll never see customer service like this in a Romanian business. The culture is too engrained against it."

His evidence? The stagnant, slow-moving lines ubiquitous in Bucharest: breadlines, lines for milk. Picking up a package at the post office took upwards of an hour. Sometimes gas stations would run out of gas, and for days you would see a standstill line of vehicles extend miles down the road. A trip to a government office—to renew a driver's license, say—led to bureaucratic goose chases that would have made Kafka proud. Even when there weren't shortages or bureaucratic roadblocks, store clerks often moved with an indifferent slowness, making sure they attended to whatever conversation they were having with a coworker first. In my father's view, Romania had many quite lovely virtues, but prompt, reliable service wasn't among them. The motto everywhere was, "They pretend to pay us, and we pretend to work."

In contrast, McDonald's workers rushed back and forth, worker bees fulfilling orders, cleaning tables, emptying the trash. No one stood still. Rude indifference? Completely absent. All cashiers smiled. They handled orders promptly. You walked out with your meal in a few minutes. Everyone received exactly what they ordered, and McDonald's never ran out of supplies. Most important, the queues never once stopped moving forward. A well-oiled machine: This seemed at the time momentous. History in the making.

I don't want to give McDonald's undue credit for political and economic forces beyond their scope, or to deny Romanians their role in changing their own country (after all, they probably hated the queue as much as my father did, for better reasons). Perhaps the best we can say is that the opening of McDonald's represents a symbolic end to the Soviet-era queue. Now that it is dead, people

Recommended Waiting-Room Reading

THE QUEUE, BY VLADIMIR SOROKIN

In this strange, funny little novel, Sorokin elegantly captures (in satirically exaggerated fashion) what it was like to live a life of never-ending line standing. The events of the novel happen all in the course of one exceedingly long line, which lasts an entire day, an entire night, and into the next morning. The novel is told in nothing but dialogue, from hundreds of characters, so that the people in line take on a kind of undifferentiated communal voice. These voices tell jokes, share gossip, and endlessly kvetch about sore feet, a hot sun, and the rising costs of consumer goods. No one knows exactly what's being sold. The front of the line seems to always be moving further away from the people in the back, as people cut in line, the store employees go on break, or the store temporarily runs out of provisions. The novel, first published in 1985, was banned by the Russian authorities, who were also known to censor any mention of the glaringly obvious news that lines in Russia were long.

BLOCKADE DIARY, BY LIDIYA GINZBURG

An amalgam of memoir and novel, the humane and beautifully written *Blockade Diary* comes from Ginzburg's memories of the siege of Leningrad. The two-and-a-half-year siege was perhaps the most harrowing event in all of Russia's harrowing history. Nearly a million and a half people died—most of them women and children—often due to starvation. Hours-long waits for bread and other provisions became extremely common, and people waited fully aware that the shop would probably run out before it was their turn to order, or close in fear of the next bombing. What other choice did they have? "The psychology of the queue," Ginzburg writes, "is based on a tense, wearing anxiety to reach the end, an inward urging-forward of empty time; this weariness excludes anything else that might relieve it." What results is "just misery, a punishment." She also offers many insights into the differences between male and female queuers in Leningrad, noting that men were far more likely to barge into the front of the line: "A man in a queue feels like a stray individual, a woman is the representative of a collective." It's the women of Leningrad, then, who inevitably take on the job of policing the queue of queue jumpers, because they speak for the community as a whole.

THE LINE, BY OLGA GRUSHIN

A famous composer who has been exiled for many years is rumored to be returning to Soviet era Russia for a final concert. Based only on this rumor, a large line begins to form at the doors of a mysterious kiosk that never seems to be open. They proceed to wait there an entire year, holding out hope. Grushin (who was born in Moscow in 1971 but emigrated to the U.S. as a child) tells us in the afterword that she based her dreamlike novel on a real-life incident: In 1962, eighty-year-old Igor Stravinsky was allowed by the Soviet authorities to return to Russia in order to conduct a valedictory concert. "The line for tickets," Grushin reports, "began a year before the performance and evolved into a unique and complex social system, with people working together and taking turns standing in line. After a year of waiting, an eighty-four-year-old cousin of Stravinsky was unable to attend, as the tickets had sold out; her number in the line was 5,001."

(anthropologists, sociologists, artists) are asking: What exactly was the Soviet queue?

It's been estimated that during the Cold War, Russians spent nearly a third of their average day standing in a line of one sort or another (all told, 80 billion hours a year!). It was considered normal to take off work for a couple hours simply in order to queue. How could this fail to have a massive influence on Russian and Eastern European culture? It was the subject of folklore, jokes, songs, poetry, street art, novels, plays, anecdotes from travel guides (not to mention its rhetorical use in our own country up into the present, as in the cryptic rants your loony uncle writes on the subject of "Obama's creeping socialism" on Facebook). In the

1970s and '80s, while young children in America—known to playact the things they see adults do—played house or cops and robbers, Russian children were witnessed playing the saddest make-believe I can imagine, a game called In the Queue.

The Soviet ethos of line standing from the beginning was partly practical (because people gotta wait somehow) and partly ideological in nature. The act of standing in line had been sporadic at best in czarist Russia at the turn of the twentieth century, but it snowballed into existence in the lead-up to the revolution in 1917, as workers began to organize themselves into a collective movement. After the revolution, the queue was inscribed into the DNA of the new government, which organized itself into bureaus with chains of command (always ripe breeding grounds for lines). The queue was further reinforced by rapid industrialization, urbanization, and the subsequent hard, lean years of regular food shortages under Lenin's various Five Year Plans.

What do dictators do when people begin to grumble about the long waits? First, deny that waits are too long and censor anyone who says they are. Second, anoint the queue with a rich mythology. State-sponsored poets invited the Muse to sing the virtues—sometimes even the heroism—of waiting in line. The queue became a symbol of Communism itself. The line stander heroically denies his own self-interests for the sake of the community. Due to the shape of the line, the line stander becomes future-oriented: not now, but in time. They were heroically suffering in this life for a bright Soviet future to come—in its more material way, not unlike the promises of Christianity, which has its saints and sinners line up at the pearly gates after a lifetime of hardship and toil. A bit of folklore about Lenin has it that he once insisted on waiting his turn in line at a barbershop, despite everyone insisting he go first. "We have to respect queues and orderliness," Lenin beatifically says. "We made the laws ourselves after all." And so even saintly Lenin waited his turn.

Such a mythology goes only so far to disguise the quotidian reality: a corrupt, mismanaged and highly inefficient government bureaucracy that controlled both industry and the state, and micromanaged the lives of its citizens, while ensuring its officials the sorts of goods and services average citizens went without. Want to take a vacation in another part of the country? Better go to the appropriate bureau and run a request chit up the chain of command. Want to buy a car or move to a bigger apartment? Put your name on a list. For bigger ticket items, just don't be surprised if you have to wait a few months or years—decades even, in some cases—to get what you came for. The front of this virtual line disappears into a nebulous, abstract future (in the local taxonomy of waiting, they called these phenomena "invisible queues").

Meanwhile, in the case of your more everyday consumer goods, the Soviet political elite decided what state-approved products were made in what state-run factories, and which state-run stores these products would be sold in. Supply chains often lacked rhyme or reason. Do customers need potatoes, umbrellas, and toothpaste? Too bad, but we do have shipments of mealy apples, rubber boots, and tins of anchovies coming your way sometime next week.

Which leads to another type within the Soviet queue taxonomy: in the genus of shortage queues, the species known as the spontaneous queue, *Linea voluntaria*. An old Romanian joke gives a good example:

A man stumbles home after a night of heavy drinking but then falls asleep in a doorway. When he wakes up, a line has formed that extends around the block. He asks the old woman behind him why they're all standing there.

"Well, we saw you waiting here and figured there must be something for sale." He says no, he just fell asleep there, and now he's going home to sleep it off.

He takes a few steps but sees that no one else makes a

move. He asks the woman, "Why aren't you leaving?
I said I only fell asleep."
   "What, and lose my place in line?"

Behind the Iron Curtain, citizens became foragers.
The problem was not so much having money, but having
little you could buy with that money. Because there was
little chance that a store would have what you need when
you needed it, you picked up whatever you could find and
stockpiled it.

If while walking down the street you see a line outside
a store, don't hesitate. Get in line first, and then ask the
person in front of you what they're selling. Don't particularly need a gallon of lighter fluid, tins of shoe polish, some
typewriter ribbon? Someone might. An underground
economy of stockpiled goods (their prices handsomely
inflated) flourished. Neighbors bartered what they had
for what they needed. In Romania up through the 1990s,
everyone carried cloth grocery bags everywhere, bunched
up in their coat pockets. You didn't want to miss an opportunity. I carried one myself sometimes: Even children were
enlisted in the hunt, and often family members would play
relay for each other if the lines were too long.

Propaganda painted the line stander as selfless, noble.
In reality, Machiavellian tactics thrived. A line could be the

Bored Games

In 2011, the Polish Institute of National Remembrance released a beautifully produced board game called Kolejka (Polish for "queue") that I keep in a prominent place on my board-game shelf (you can find an international version for sale in the U.S.). In the game, players line up their avatars in front of a series of shops (the clothing store, the grocery store, the furniture store, and so forth). These avatars then jockey for better places in line, using tactics that would be familiar to a resident of Poland during the Cold War. The queue jumper. The woman who uses her child as an excuse to go to the front. The friend in the Worker's Part Provincial Committee who tips you off about the delivery schedule. The person who draws up a "community list" for a virtual queue. Et cetera. The player who gets all the items on her shopping list wins.

The game was created in order to teach children—too young to have experienced Soviet hardships firsthand—about some of the difficulties of life under Communism, and the player's manual offers instructive historical context for the game. Unfortunately, I think the game perhaps sends a mixed message: It is surprisingly enjoyable to play, considering the subject matter. Kids might take away the wrong lesson.

place of discrete and bitter battles, full of savage (if low-scale) Realpolitik: temporary alliances, tense standoffs and truces, subterfuge, seized opportunities, behavior as ruthless as that of any self-interested capitalist. Queuing, after all, was complicated, and complication favors those willing and able to game the system. For instance, any line was actually made of two lines, one for regular folk and one for those unable to stand so long: the elderly, the disabled, women who were pregnant or had small children. So know anyone with a screaming baby you can borrow?

People cut when they thought they could get away with it. If someone had a relationship with a store employee or a state official, you can bet they would try to exploit that. They bought and sold places in line and held spots for their friends and family. Groups banded together to protect their places. The phenomenon of professional line standing flourished. When lines can regularly last for hours or days, strange local rules of arbitration sprang up. In Poland, for instance, unofficial "queuers' committees" formed to keep the peace. They signed people up for waiting lists and made each person on that list stand for an assigned period of time. The line stander could then leave the spot, reporting several times a day for roll call.

But line standing was not always all desperate jockeying. Russian novelist Vladimir Sorokin, for instance, remembers the queue as a ritual, a "quasi-surrogate for church": "Gray and boring, but inescapable, the line dissected the body into pieces, pacified and disciplined it, gave time to think about the advantages of socialism and about the class struggle; and in the end they were rewarded with food and goods." He fondly remembers a period in the 1970s when obtaining food wasn't an issue; people could devote their time queueing for items that weren't so desperately needed, like imported American jeans. "They waited happily, with humor," he reports, "in a familial atmosphere that was even rather cozy." A family sometimes bickers and grumbles. But it also imparts a collective self-identity, a spirit of togetherness.

If the average queue was church, the line to Lenin's tomb was Mecca, the pilgrimage the Russian citizen could be dutifully expected to perform voluntarily at least once in his or her lifetime. The hours-long wait was as part of the sacramental ritual as seeing Lenin's embalmed body. If you visited Red Square anytime between Lenin's death in 1924 and into the 1990s (and to a lesser extent into the present) you would see this line, rain or shine, snow or sleet. Here was the queue that contained all queues, the body and blood of Soviet queuing and of the Communist experiment in general. "But of this I am sure," the Russian poet A. V. Gusev wrote in 1960, "In one hundred years time / Here a queue will still stand at the Moscow mausoleum."

He was wrong to be so sure. In 1990, McDonald's opened in Pushkin Square, only a few blocks away. As both Russian and foreign commentators were quick to note, for once the line to Lenin's mausoleum had met its match: The queue in Red Square seemed to dwindle, even while thousands upon thousands waited patiently for their Big Mac. The line to McDonald's dwarfed the line to see Lenin by three to one, by some reports. A tidal wave of Western imports—and stores to buy them in—followed in short order. What happens when you are confronted by the fact that, as Vladimir Sorokin puts it, "there are not 3 kinds of sausage, but 33. Or even 333"? Existential crises, is what. Not many Russians remember the 1990s as being a particularly easy decade to live through.

"When the new stores opened," Sorokin writes, "not with 333, but only 10 types of sausage, the line split up into 10 small lines. It turned out that people could choose their sausage. The Soviet line couldn't handle the ordeal of choice." The change happened in a remarkably small number of years. My father was right about McDonald's, it turns out. In Russia, soon there were hardly any lines at all, simply clusters of self-interested individuals trying to get ahead of the pack.

Today, you see hardly any queues there whatsoever. The Soviet line collapsed; an important part of a nation's collective identity was lost. Some wonder today whether that loss was too heavy.

WAITING FOR A BIG MAC IN CHINA

At least for the first week, the wait time at Moscow's first McDonald's gave Russians time to review the how-to manuals provided to them by McDonald's employees. How to order, what to order, what to do after paying. Please bus your own tables. No, you don't eat a Big Mac by peeling it apart layer by layer. Et cetera. Sometimes during peak hours, a female employee would stand outside with a bullhorn, warning the customers: "The employees inside will smile at you. This does not mean that they are laughing at you. We smile because we are happy to serve you." Smiles: another scarce commodity in the Soviet Union. (In scowls, however, they were world leaders.)

A McDonald's employee needs training. So does the customer. The fast-food industry exists because of an essential trade-off: McDonald's feeds you promptly and cheaply, and in exchange you agree to deflect some of their labor costs. You carry your own tray. You fill your own soda cup. You seat yourself. You clear your own table. The agreement also implicitly stipulates that you wait your turn, order quickly, eat quickly, and then get the hell out, because someone else is behind you and needs your table:

This is the McDonald's way. They've got billions to serve, after all. When you don't know what you're doing, you gum up the works. Eastern Europe, at least, had the queue down pat. But what happens in countries that don't?

In 2007, a curious item from Reuters popped up in some news feeds: "Beijing Institutes Queueing Day." This was in the lead-up to the 2008 Summer Olympics: The People's Republic of China, the article said, wanted its citizens to be on their best behavior. National Voluntarily Wait-in-Line Day was one weapon in a larger arsenal; the battle was getting the Chinese to act "civilized" (their word, not mine). The powers-that-be wanted to project a wholesome image of China to the world. The Office of Capital Ethics Development—which has also run campaigns against littering, spitting in public, and the use of skimpily-clad models at auto shows—instituted the monthly holiday. The office then uses a "civic index" to measure improved behavior. (It is happy to note, for instance, that the index jumped from 65.21 percent in 2005 to 69.06 percent in 2006. I have no idea what those numbers could possibly mean, or how they were calculated.)

"Where there are more than two people," read the official announcement, "they should wait in line." Expats and tourists to China, who in dispatches home often complain about the lack of queue etiquette, might rejoice at this development. So might middle-class Chinese. The overcrowded conditions of many of China's cities has not been helped by the fact that until recently no concerted effort has been made to train residents how best to use the modern city.

On YouTube videos, for instance, you can see the prevailing stratagems for boarding a subway car in Beijing: Everyone stands as close as possible to one another. If there is any gap in the crowd, command and conquer. Move into the breach. People have to fight their way out of the subway as much as they have to fight their way in. Where lines are enforced, people still squeeze in incredibly tightly, pressed against one another, as if afraid that otherwise someone might slip into the gap. Even in places where standing in line is a voluntary phenomenon—cosmopolitan Beijing, for instance—the line cutter is a distressingly common phenomenon.

Whoever chose the eleventh of every month to observe Queueing Day was inspired: 11 resembles two people standing in a line. (By a similar logic, the twenty-second of every month was named National Voluntarily Give Up Your Seat on the Bus Day. The 2 is supposed to be a person sitting, from the country that brought the world ideograms.) The Capital Ethics Development Office plastered bus stations everywhere with signs, variations on a theme: "I wait in line and am cultured. I display courtesy and am happy." Or: "It's civilized to queue, it's glorious to be polite." Or: "Voluntarily wait in line, be polite and put others first." Or: "I care about and participate in the Olympics and set an example by queueing." Or (my favorite for its spare elegance): "I am a member of the queue."

Did the campaign work? At least one day a month it did. On the eleventh, Beijing residents (I'm told) exhibited some preeminently straight and well-disciplined lines. I don't know whether or not on the twelfth people returned to the established modus operandi of crowding.

I'd wager that China will find its way, and perhaps the increasing presence of companies like McDonald's will help. This is all part of a process we've seen many times before, in all parts of the globe. China is in the midst of unprecedented economic growth. Spurred by new industries and international trading, the cities are growing at exponential rates, drawing in people from all around, many of whom have no set idea of how to behave in a city, especially in social situations where no rules have yet been established. In the United States, Miss Manners columns were once the rage; our early silent movies often made fun of our hick country cousins who didn't know how to behave in the city. A national culture seeks (and sometimes

Greed Is Good—Sometimes

Sometimes, in other countries, the opposite of "acting civilized" has been actively courted. In the 1970s, the government of Singapore encouraged behavior known as *kiasu,* vernacular Chinese meaning roughly "fear of losing."

Perhaps anticipating the 1980s mantra "Greed is good," the term is used to describe getting ahead at all costs, regardless of social ceremony. This includes taking more food than you can eat at the buffet, not holding the door open for someone, cutting in line, and so on. These are done while avoiding all eye contact, to avoid social shame.

The idea was that if you want to be a success—and therefore make Singapore a success in the process—it's up to you, so be greedy, be rude, be selfish. It was a way of turning Singapore into an economic powerhouse, without the government having to become a universal provider to its citizens. Ayn Rand would be proud.

Now that Singapore is the East Asian titan it sought to be, the government is trying to curb this behavior somewhat through "politeness campaigns"—after all, traffic becomes a bit messy when everyone refuses to adopt the "zipper in" approach to merging, and metros run slower when every stop results in a riot of selfish go-getters pushing and shoving.

The *kiasu* mind-set was brought to the world's

attention in 2000, when McDonald's became the center of a national crisis. Improbably, the crisis involved a Hello Kitty doll promotion they ran, which created a frenzy. Apparently Hello Kitty is insanely popular in Singapore. At times, roughly 300,000 people—a full 8 percent of Singapore's total population!—turned out to queue up in front of Singapore's 114 franchises.

For the five weeks of the promotion, these queues became a battlefield. People were regularly cutting in line, quarreling, brawling, vandalizing local property, and engaging in other forms of rioting usually associated with drunken soccer fans after a big match. The Singapore government was forced to weigh in on the episode, chastising McDonald's for their lack of foresight and calling for them to do something about the problem. McDonald's eventually hired private security to enforce the queues before finally cutting the promotion short by a week.

stumbles) to find a way—by carrot, by stick, or by both at once—to tame its crowds.

China might look within its own border for precedent—in Hong Kong, which is the one place in China where the weary traveler might find a respite from the constant crush of people desperate to get ahead of one another. There, people politely wait their turn wherever you go, and glower with prim dismay when their visiting mainland cousins—allowed to freely travel to Hong Kong since the British gave up the colony in 1997—barge rudely into the front of the line. And whom do many Hong Kong residents credit for their own firm grasp of queueing etiquette? That's right: McDonald's. The opening of McDonald's there in 1975 is one of the foundational myths of the middle class. It answers the question *Why do we behave so well?*

Is this true? Like all foundational myths, the truth is complicated. Yes, the tight, jostling scrum was the standard before the late '70s. And yes, McDonald's was one of the first businesses in Hong Kong to enforce queueing standards, in part by hiring queue monitors during peak hours. (The distinction of the first company to enforce the line, however, goes to the Kowloon Motor Bus Company, which in the 1960s constructed queue barriers to funnel passengers between the concourse and their buses.) But the story is really one of an increasingly powerful middle class—created, in part, by the very market forces that are creating a middle class in mainland China today—that became aware of itself as such and imprinted its values on the wider populace.

Before the 1970s, Hong Kong was a city of immigrants: The majority of residents were refugees who had swarmed in waves from other parts of China during previous decades. Like any city that goes through a period of unprecedented growth, no established decorum existed at first: Everyone's traditions were different, leading to confusion and chaos, where everyone worked at cross-purposes with one another.

But these immigrants had children, and these children were Hong Kong residents through and through. McDonald's was introduced at a time when these children of immigrants (now becoming solidly middle-class residents) were coming into their own as a social force. Hong Kong was already steadily moving toward becoming more civilized (which is partly to say Westernized). McDonald's only taught the middle class a particular social formation by which one might become more respectable, more civilized (to use the classic term, more bourgeois).

In mainland China today, we can see how this process plays out by looking at people's relation to McDonald's. In 1992, McDonald's opened its first restaurant in Beijing (in—a typically brilliant move of American corporate agit-prop—Tiananmen Square). Now the company has several thousand franchises throughout China. These restaurants are universally popular among the Chinese, many of whom go there almost as a social rite. But two facts make this popularity seem counterintuitive. One: McDonald's is fairly expensive in relation to the average salary in China, at least compared with local dining options. Two: Many

Chinese don't really much care for the taste of McDonald's food. So why would anyone eat there?

In short? Chinese citizens go for the prestige and the education. They publicly display their own Westernness in the eyes of others, simply by showing that they, too, know how to be in a McDonald's. Here's how the West gets in line, here's how the West orders, here's how the West eats. Sometimes parents will take their child to McDonald's and simply hover over him while he eats. Later, the parents will go eat someplace else that's cheaper and tastes better to them. But that child? Who knows? Maybe the know-how of eating a Big Mac will make that crucial difference when applying to medical school. The child is being socialized into the ways of the wider world. Those parents are making an investment into their child's future well-being.

The Office of Capital Ethics Development seeks to "civilize" China (ironic, considering that China is the oldest civilization on earth). Its goal is to make Chinese citizens "missionaries of civilization" (to quote the director of the office). Where you eat, what you eat, how you eat, how you wait for the things you eat: In any country, class, refinement, and taste have always been part of a complex social economy by which one group (typically the middle class) seeks to impart its values on another group (typically the lower classes). In the world's second largest economy, this process plays out on an international scale, especially

The *Jay* in *Jaywalker*

Americans react strongly to public shaming too! For an equivalent, consider the word *jaywalker*. A jay was originally pejorative Midwestern slang for (roughly) "dumb loudmouthed hick." In the city, a jay was known to wander dumbly around, dazzled by glitter: bright lights, tall buildings, store windows. They were roadblocks to the streamlined path of the focused urban dweller. The term *jaywalker* was coined in 1913 when a department store in Syracuse hired a man dressed as Santa Claus (megaphone in hand) to shout insults at people who didn't cross the street properly.

Before the advent of the automobile, people used the street however they pleased; they were mainly for the use of pedestrians, after all. But when cars become more prominent in city streets, so do pedestrian fatalities. So that cities wouldn't pass laws limiting vehicle traffic, car companies began a massive PR campaign shifting the blame for these fatalities onto the pedestrians killed. The campaign was a big success. By the mid-1920s, no one wanted to look like a crude simpleton—a (gasp) jaywalker—so people began crossing at crosswalks. Cars successfully took over city streets everywhere. It has been a chore to be a pedestrian in America ever since.

when the Olympics are in town. In the U.S., even while we gained ever more economic and political power, our middle class once looked to the Old World with a sense of cultural inferiority and superficially imitated its fashions and manners. Similarly, China today looks West.

People in the West eat at McDonald's; people in China eat at McDonald's. People in the West queue; people in China (should) queue. For over a decade now, in the more cosmopolitan areas of China, waiting in line (*pai dui*, in Mandarin) carries with it a certain aura of respectability: People who *pai dui* congratulate themselves for being civilized, cosmopolitan, Westernized. Meanwhile, cutting in line (*cha dui*) is associated with backcountry bumpkins, hicks with bad teeth (people who probably can't afford McDonald's, in other words). This has happened without much government intervention, in the free market of social capital. Likely, as a new generation of middle-class residents surpasses the older immigrant generation in size, these norms will gradually take hold.

The social capital of eating at McDonald's may be the most effective way to "train" the Chinese people in the ways of Western queueing (whether or not adopting Western norms wholesale is desirable is another matter entirely). A man sees another man trying to edge his way into the front of the line. "Hey! What's the matter

Don't Trust the Lines in Japan

While people in Beijing were still dutifully practicing their line-standing skills in the lead-up to the Olympics, across the Sea of Japan a small scandal was brewing. In 2008, the McDonald's corporate branch in Japan was forced to respond to allegations that it had paid at least a thousand people to stand in line for the release of the Quarter Pounder in Osaka. These line standers were paid a thousand yen (roughly twelve dollars) an hour, plus the cost of their meal. At one point, they made up about half the people in line. McDonald's pleaded guilty the way corporations often do—by blaming the franchise owners, claiming that they had acted without official consent. The corporate branch promised never to abuse the public's trust in this manner again.

On the face of it, this would seem to be a counter-intuitive approach to marketing. Isn't the point of fast food that it's fast? Wouldn't long lines turn away paying customers? But really, this sort of thing happens all the time in Japan. A video game console is released. The Japanese news reports how many hundreds have been waiting in line for days. Only later is it revealed that a percentage of these people waiting in line were paid to do so. An up-and-coming Korean pop singer flies to Tokyo. A tabloid reports that eight hundred fans line up waiting for him at the airport, with footage suggesting a large crowd. In reality, there are really only one hundred at the airport, eighty of which were paid to be there. Et cetera. Lather, rinse, repeat.

Why is this tactic effective? Unlike China and most of the rest of East Asia, the Japanese are inveterate queuers (they make the Brits look like rank amateurs, in fact). In the aftermath of the 2011 tsunami, for instance, the Japanese received international attention for their almost complete lack of any sort of looting. Instead, everyone calmly and patiently queued up, sometimes upwards of twelve hours, waiting for supplies.

In fact, the Japanese appear to enjoy standing in line, or at least enjoy the anticipation that comes from standing in line. When offered a choice between vendor A and vendor B, each selling a similar product, a Japanese resident will choose the one with the *longer* line. It's not uncommon for people to wait several hours to get into a popular new restaurant. In Japan, the wait is part of what gives a product its value.

In Japan, fads breed and die daily, but the queue remains. Nearly every day, Japanese television features a barrage of reports from the front lines, reporting on the amount of time one has to wait to get into this or that trendy establishment. The wait time becomes an essential part of a company's promotional tools. But as we see with the case of McDonald's, this can lead to abuse. Why not simply pay people to drum up interest by standing in line? The practice is part of a long-standing tradition, dating back to the Meiji period at the turn of the last century, when department store owners would hire people to mill around in their shops. These phony line standers are called *sakura* (not to be confused with the cherry blossom of the same name). For some, this is a full-time profession.

How did the Japanese become such eager line standers? It's a difficult question to answer (not much has been written on the subject, at least in English). I would simply point out two things. The first is that, isolated on all sides by water and restrictive immigration policies, Japan is much more culturally homogeneous (and hence more culturally unified) than China or the United States could ever hope to be. More emphasis is put on the collective identity. What's best for the group is what's best for the individual.

Second, Japan industrialized much earlier than other nations in the area, starting in the late nineteenth century. Like the Chinese today, the Japanese of the Meiji period—following the fall of the shogunate in 1868—explicitly sought to civilize their populace by incorporating Western elements into their culture (in architecture, the economy, social norms and practices, and the introduction of department stores). They self-consciously turned their backs on their "hopelessly backward" Asian neighbors. (And sometimes, like many countries in the West, they used the perceived backwardness of their neighbors as an excuse to colonize them.) As we see today in China, being civilized (literally, adapted to life in cities) is a form of social with you?" he says. "Back of the line, pal." The line cutter barely has time to back away, when the man turns to his friend, points a thumb at the line cutter, and mutters just within earshot, "What an ignoramus. Can you believe this simple backward blockhead? Does he even know how to McDonald's?" What the line stander says sotto voce to his friend is more bruising than what he says directly to the line cutter; the line cutter blushes. Perhaps he'll think twice about trying to cut in line again. As the residents of Hong Kong found, a simple disapproving shake of the head may be enough to discipline the queue. Never underestimate the power of a public shaming.

Give China enough time, and perhaps there will be lines—or some other form of socially sanctioned order—at banks, at taxi stands, at cinemas, and wherever you might expect a crowd. Some future generation might even find the queue to feel commonplace and natural, mostly absent of the vexed cultural power plays of pride and shame we see today. And someday (who knows?) people there might even grow to like the taste of a Big Mac.

CHAPTER SIX

LESSONS FROM AN UNDERGROUND BUNKER

Science in the Magic Kingdom

So many belief systems, so many pilgrimages. Muslims have Mecca, of course. Christians, Muslims, and the Jewish people all claim Jerusalem as a holy site. Hindus, Buddhists, and Sikhs have their equivalent pilgrimages. Russians could be expected to perform the rite of standing in line to see Lenin's tomb, a symbolic act under Communism. In all these places, expect large crowds and long waits. Is there an equivalent pilgrimage in America, that everyone who claims to be American is expected to partake in at some point in their lives? I would argue that place is Disney World, arguably the American Mecca of hedonic consumerism, which roughly 70 percent of living Americans have visited at one point or another.

This pilgrimage will very likely lead you into the holding area for one of Disney's holiest of holies, the It's a Small World After All ride, which (as one of Disney's earliest attractions) forms the park's spiritual locus. There you will wait with several hundred others, occasionally reminding yourself that you paid good money to basically stand in lines all day. But never mind that. You're mostly having a good time. For now, steel yourself to the task at hand, which is making sure you experience It's a Small World. Why? Because you're supposed to. This is Disney World. Who goes to Disney World without seeing It's a Small World?

Finally, you're boarded onto your little river boat. The music starts. Those brightly colored dolls—dressed to reflect the abundance of cultures in the world—begin to bludgeon you with syrupy sing-a-long, the same chirrupy refrain over and over and over. . . . "It's a small world after all. . . . It's a small world after all. . . . It's a small, small world. . . ." The journey lasts eleven minutes, but it can feel endless. Over the course of it, you might be reminded of *Apocalypse Now*, a movie about another river cruise that drives a man insane. For eleven minutes, you feel you're living in a fever dream.

SPONTANEITY ON A SCHEDULE

But the ride does end. At last you disembark, stumbling into blinding Florida sunlight, the song trailing away behind you. Now, having paid your respect to the mouse—honoring the original vision of Walt Disney—you are free to jet off toward more pleasurable pleasures, an abundance of rides spread across multiple parks. But a part of the It's a Small World ride sticks with you throughout the day: that maddening little earworm of a song, repeating itself like a skipping record in your head. "It's a small world after all. . . . It's a small, small world. . . ."

Yes, a small world. It does seem these days that all parts of the world are at remarkably close quarters. Nowhere does this appear truer than in the Magic Kingdom, in which a Bavarian castle, an Old West mining town, and an African jungle are all within a few minutes' walking distance from one another. But more than that, Disney World is simply crowded. On any given day, thousands upon thousands from all over the world will descend upon the Orlando area in a gloriously colorful mass. It's estimated that around 18 million people visit the park each year. This means an average of 47,000 are in the park each day (and a good deal more than that during peak season).

If two's a party, and three's a crowd, 47,000 is a fiasco in waiting. Those numbers have all the makings of the world's biggest daily bottleneck. And yet everything seems to go OK. Actually, it works magnificently. There are few scuffles, zero stampedes. People aren't falling over each other like Keystone Cops. Few seem lost or fretful or angry. Nobody is exploding into fits of queue rage. Yes, it's a small world. But it avoids most of the pitfalls of over-congestion that we've seen elsewhere. Somehow we all fit. The lines keep moving. Nothing grinds to a dead halt.

Nearly everyone comes away satisfied, despite the long lines. For me, therein lies the real magic of the Magic Kingdom: It's a small world that's somehow just big enough.

What's the source of this magic? If you're like me, part of the pleasure of Disney World is marveling at how it achieves the illusions it does. I enjoy the rides and the shows while I'm there, sure. But at the same time, I want to lift the lid and peer inside. How does this whole thing work, anyway? Where are the secret tunnels, the command centers? What's behind those impeccable facades? The theme park feels like a marvelous contraption with millions of moving parts. It is elegant in its complexity and nearly flawless in its execution. And not least among its many marvels is the way that Disney subtly, often imperceptibly, manages its crowds and keeps gridlock to a minimum.

Disney runs smoothly through meticulous attention to detail, by understanding how crowds operate, and by designing the park accordingly. The park's operators may create the illusion of spontaneity, but make no mistake: Theirs is spontaneity on a schedule, tightly regulated and controlled.

Unfortunately, there's no magic to the Magic Kingdom. Keeping the crowd content is a science.

IT'S A SMALL WORLD

The problems involved in managing crowds are not unique to Disney, of course. Since the crowd was first recognized as a social force in the late nineteenth century, there have been those who have sought to study it and control it, not least in the realm of business. Any business that serves customers directly will sometimes suffer the slings and arrows of uncertain customer turnout.

How does a business owner know when a crowd is going to show up? When is there likely to be a bottleneck? How many people does one need to employ, for how long, and for which hours of the day?

Wouldn't it be nice to predict the future? Unfortunately, there's no exact way to say when a crowd will appear or how large it will be. If more people show up than anticipated and the business owner doesn't have enough workers on shift to handle them all, a line forms. Customers complain or, worse yet, go elsewhere for their needs to be met.

At the same time, a business can't simply hire an army of workers on the off chance that a large crowd will show up. Employees are expensive.

Any successful business must strike a balance between perfect customer satisfaction and the bottom line. All businesses must do this to be competitive. Sometimes businesses offer enticements to draw people to come at certain times rather than others. Bars do this with happy hours, for example. By reducing the price of their drinks at times that are usually dead, they maximize profits for those hours and help level the crush of customers during busier times.

Ideally, businesses want to create a small world that's just large enough, neither more nor less. Disney is the uncontested master of this balance, using the most state-of-the-art technologies. It would have to be. No one *needs* to visit a theme park. Attendance is strictly voluntary. The line to get onto the Dumbo ride is not the same as the breadline during a famine. Disney must ensure that it remains "the happiest place on earth," while maximizing the bottom line by avoiding any slack.

How do you make sure that nearly all 47,000 of the park's daily visitors aren't swarming Space Mountain at once, for instance, when the Jungle Cruise remains relatively unused? How many hours should the park be open in the off-season versus the peak season? How quickly can you pack people onto the Dumbo ride and get them off again? How many boats should you send through The Pirates of the Caribbean every hour? How much of a discount should you give diners who choose to take their lunch at off-peak times? Everything counts. An employee who, say, leaves seats on It's a Small World unloaded—thereby decreasing efficiency—creates an imbalance in the system, leading to bottlenecks and longer lines elsewhere in the park.

The science that can start to answer questions like these began in the early twentieth century, when it was becoming apparent that the world was indeed growing smaller. New forms of travel and communication meant that the world was interconnected in ways unthinkable before. Cities grew ever more congested, with more people using resources from fewer sources. Once hundreds of people might have used the village well; in a major city, the metropolitan municipal waterworks might serve millions. As you can imagine, this concentration also increases the possibility of gridlock.

It was that most modern of early twentieth-century technologies that necessitated the study of waiting in line: the telephone. In 1903, the Copenhagen Telephone Company decided it needed to address an issue that plagued the rollout of telephones in many countries: namely, traffic congestion, long waiting lists for getting a subscription, and (most important) vociferous customer complaints. The familiar slapstick image of the harried switchboard operator in many midcentury films, struggling to keep up with the flood of phone calls and getting tied up in the cables, was born out of these problems. How many operators does the phone company need to employ to keep up with traffic? How many phone calls could the telephone company expect during any given hour? How do we keep harried switchboard operators from becoming entangled in wires?

The Copenhagen Telephone Company established a laboratory to study these problems, hiring Danish mathematician Agner Krarup Erlang, who in 1909 published "The Theory of Probability and Telephone Conversations." This is considered the first study in what would later be called queueing theory. The paper—along with subsequent ones—had an enormous impact. It was so important that a researcher in America's own preeminent telephone laboratory, AT&T's Bell Labs, purportedly taught himself Danish so that he could better understand it.

Erlang's study translated the problem of queues into a mathematical language modeled on what's called a Poisson distribution (named after French mathematician Siméon

Denis Poisson). What Erlang (and Poisson before him) was looking for was probabilities. What is the likelihood of x number of people using the telephone at 3 o'clock in the afternoon? Unfortunately, fortune tellers don't exist. There's no way to predict precise numbers. But using Poisson distribution, we can calculate the probability of x number of events happening within a certain interval of time and/or space, based on the known average of those number of events.

If we know, for instance, that there is an average of one hundred callers between the hours of eight and nine a.m., and those calls last (on average) three minutes, a mathematician using Poisson distribution can then calculate the probability of there only being ten callers (somewhat unlikely), ninety callers (likely), or three thousand callers (highly unlikely). Using this knowledge, the phone company can decide how many switches and switchboard operators are needed from eight to nine a.m.

Theoretically, it's possible that every single one of Copenhagen's telephone users could attempt to use the telephone at the same time—just as it's theoretically possible that every living human within driving distance of Orlando could decide to descend upon Disney World en masse, creating the logjam to end all logjams. But the odds of this happening are infinitesimal, bordering on the impossible. It would be unwise—and extremely costly—for companies to base their daily operating procedures on this possibility. But we do see situations that sometimes come close. For instance, people have noted the drop in water pressure during Super Bowl commercials: This is a real (though exaggerated) phenomenon, caused by too many people using the toilet at once. And if you try to use your telephone following a disaster, such as a tornado, you might find that your call is dropped: an example of too many people trying to call for help or to reassure concerned loved ones at once.

The next question queue theory seeks to answer is how best to work through the assembled line. "Best" here depends on what you mean the line to do. It can mean what is most efficient, what is fairest, what is least costly, or what keeps the customer most content. Because not all queues function the same way, to study queues mathematically means more strictly defining the parameters and workings of the notoriously hard-to-define queue.

Queue theorists establish the number of potential customers there are, called in queue-theory parlance the *source* (for instance, the sum total of Copenhagen Telephone Company subscribers or the sum total of people within driving distance of Disney World). They take into account the number of servers, and the average amount of time each service takes. They must establish the *queue discipline*, meaning the rules for deciding who's next. Of course, everyone knows first come, first served (which queue theorists call FIFO, first in, first out). But there may be good reason to employ a different discipline, such as "priority" queues, "last in, first out" (LIFO) queues, "service-in-random-order" (SIRO) queues, or shortest-job-first queues.

By creating a model, one can test for a number of things. Which model will cost a company less? How long are customers likely to wait in this model versus that one? Which model is fairer? What model will best handle spikes in traffic? Do the math. Run the test. Queue theory doesn't seek to prescribe any one way of doing business. There may be good reasons not to adopt the most efficient model (I think consumers would be pretty angry if a company were to employ a last in, first out queue, for instance, even if that were the most efficient choice). But it's helpful to know why and how lines form and to have strategies in place for addressing them when they do.

Queue theory is a science that's been applied to everything from theme parks to traffic congestion, delivering mail, and how best to board an airplane (which—surprise!—airlines don't do particularly well). Nowhere is its influence more evident than the world of computing and the Internet, which exists only because of programming that orders actions, tasks, and processes according to deliberately chosen sequences (in other words, according to a queueing discipline). The local Copenhagen phone traffic that Erlang studied has metamorphosed into the global Internet, different only in scale and complexity, where millions of users vie for limited bandwidth that must be capacious enough to handle spikes in traffic. (In many ways, the ongoing battle for Net neutrality—whose partisans object to letting Internet providers charge certain companies for priority service—is a battle over queue discipline as well as a battle over what's fair.)

In fact, much queueing goes on precisely so you no longer have to. What's changed is what's doing the queueing. People still queue, of course. But so does data. So do the objects you purchase in the store, which line up one before the next on the shelf. So do tasks that you complete. For instance, when I procrastinate, opting to do the dishes before finishing my taxes—choosing the easier of two unpleasant tasks—I am unconsciously making a decision that can be analyzed according to queueing theory (I am choosing a "shortest job first" discipline).

In our daily lives, few of us mathematically analyze the way we spend our time. After all, we don't have the resources to hire a small army of mathematicians and

The Americanization of the Queue

We see the influence of queuing theory on the language of computing, and the influence of computing language on our own, in the growing use of the word *queue* in America. I remember encountering the word in books by English authors when I was younger and considering it an exotic Britishism, like spelling *colour* with a *u.* Now it seems to be everywhere.

What accounts for the change? According to Alice Robb of *The New Republic,* we can blame Netflix. The DVD mailing service—which has now moved largely to online viewing—asked users to create a queue of the movies they wanted mailed to them. Initially, many users were perplexed by the word. Early on, Netflix customer service would receive calls from people asking, "What's my kway-way?" Because the word was novel enough, and because Netflix had a wide enough base of subscribers, it stuck, entering the average American lexicon, at least regarding our online activities. Now other companies, like YouTube and Amazon, use the word. Even now that Netflix has dropped their "queue" in favor of the more workman-like and more accurate (at least for online viewing) "list," it's hard not to associate the word with the company.

operations researchers to construct models for how best to structure our day for maximum efficiency. If we did, we'd probably find that we are terribly inefficient. I know I am. We make choices based on hunch and whim, not according to any ordered operation. Queues and queue theory exist to respond to the spontaneity of our choices: After all, would long lines exist if we all could—to a person—agree to coordinate our schedules?

Short of that, the best we can hope for are scientists who study our movement patterns for us and make design choices accordingly. As the saying goes, it's like herding cats

LESSONS FROM AN UNDERGROUND BUNKER

There's no magic to the Magic Kingdom. If you want to know what really makes Disney tick, you need to go underground.

The Disney Operational Command Center lies underneath that most central and visible of Disney landmarks, Cinderella Castle. The name makes it sound like a military operation, which it resembles. There, Disney workers carefully monitor the state of the queues in real time, using computers, video feed, and digital maps. From computer screens, technicians watch current wait times lit up in traffic light colors, from green to yellow to the dreaded red—meaning standstill. Using that knowledge, they can act appropriately. Are people yawning uncontrollably in the line to ride the Magic Teacups, for instance? Send in Goofy this minute to entertain them (I like to imagine there's a giant red button they can push).

They are armed with the best data analysis possible. They must first roughly determine how big the crowd will be, using the number of flight and hotel room reservations, as well as customer data from previous years, which through Poisson distribution gives them a good idea of crowd levels for the current year. They know which rides people tend to gravitate toward at which time of day, based on park layout and the popularity of each ride. This tells them, for instance, how many boats will be needed at the It's a Small World ride at any given time. And if the line becomes unusually long—the probability of which is calculable—actively tracking the situation allows them to call up a manager, telling him to launch more boats.

Meanwhile, they do their best to make sure people are evenly distributed around the park. The Haunted Mansion could be crammed while the Dumbo ride remains relatively unused close by. Not only will this annoy visitors, but it's also an example of poor park efficiency, maldistribution in what's supposed to be the smallest world possible. How do they steer crowds toward emptier parts of the park?

One thing they might do, for instance, is call for a mini-parade of Disney characters—called "Move it! Shake it! Celebrate it!"—to entice guests into underused areas in the park. Their FastPass system (and now their FastPass+ system) was also designed to better control crowd movement. Instead of blindly going where your whim drives you—a whim that theoretically might be shared with 47,000 others—you can make a reservation that moves you into the priority queue, but only at an appointed time likelier to be less busy. Knowing that his reservation is secured, the guest is free to explore less populated areas of the park.

Monitoring the cameras, the Command Center calls the shots, responding to queueing crises, establishing how many ride operators are needed at a given hour or how many cars should be in operation. Meanwhile, the crowd is herded by subtle tactics and behaves (for the most part) voluntarily. One of the biggest innovations of the original park was its single entrance. The model of earlier parks was the county fair, with entry anywhere. The lone entrance led early skeptics to doubt Walt Disney's vision, but by creating a choke point that everyone must pass through, you better understand their movement into the park.

At all points, the visitor is given directions that prescribe movement, whether by signs, by disembodied prerecorded voices, or by enthusiastic park staff. There are barriers everywhere—sometimes disguised as aesthetic objects—that limit choice of movement. Other features—a fountain, a flower garden—are meant either to attract or repel visitors to or from certain areas of the park. (What child comes to Disney World to look at a friggin' flower garden? A flower garden communicates, *Keep moving. There ain't nothing to see here.*) There never seem to be security guards anywhere until someone violates established etiquette. But try cutting into line. Guards will mysteriously appear out of nowhere to usher the rule breaker into an undisclosed location—but quietly; they wouldn't want to ruin the atmosphere by being brusque.

The name of the game throughout is throughput, the technical term for the rate by which something can be processed (data through a computer server, for instance). In this case, the throughput is guests. What's the system capacity? How many hundreds of people can a ride process per hour, from the minute they step into line, to the minute they exit the ride? If the term *throughput* seems exceedingly cold, technical, mechanical—aren't we all individual unique snowflakes, here in the happiest place on earth?—that's because it is. From an engineering standpoint, we are all just numbers, items on the assembly line, heads of cattle (though heads of cattle that they very much want to return to the park).

Keeping the Customer Happy

Disney, more than any other company that I'm aware of, has mastered the lessons that David Maister outlines in "The Psychology of Waiting Lines."

Unlike other theme parks, which indifferently put out cold metal stanchions in switchback fashion, the line-standing area at Disney World is itself "themed." This both separates it from other areas of the park, and makes it feel like a part of the ride itself (because "people want to get started").

Separating the queueing area from the rest of the park also masks how long the line truly is. The line is hidden, so that people don't feel turned off by what they perceive as an impossibly long line. Many queueing areas are designed so that you can never see more than a few people in front of you. They twist back and forth like any airport security line, which helps conserve space, but each segment of the line is invisible from any other segment (because "anxiety makes waits seem longer").

Once in line, visitors might entertain themselves by reading the inscriptions on the tombs outside of the Haunted House, for instance, or playing video games while waiting for Space Mountain, or interacting with the "next-gen" queue at the Winnie-the-Pooh ride, which allows children to play around in the 100 Acre Wood while they wait (because "occupied time feels shorter than unoccupied time").

At the head of every line, there is an electronic sign that gives an estimated wait time (because "uncertain waits are longer than known, finite waits"). These wait times are nearly always inflated so that people feel they are moving more quickly than predicted and to give Disney some wiggle room if something goes wrong.

Disney features separate (and generally much quicker) lines for guests who are visiting by themselves. This lets them more efficiently fill seats (it's much easier to find one seat than five together) and keep the solo visitor's disquiet to a minimum (because "solo waits feel longer than group waits").

While Disney does feature priority queues, through its FastPass system, they are free with the price of admission. Anyone can use the FastPass reservation, based on first come, first served. No one pays extra to get to the front of the line (because "unfair waits are longer than equitable waits").

These adaptations developed piecemeal over the course of the park's history. Walt Disney was by all reports extremely interested in how Disney guests experienced their wait. He would often personally study the lines, take pictures of the lines, and think of ways to improve the line-standing experience. He encouraged his engineers to stand in them as well, experience them for themselves, and talk to people in the crowd. When the park opened, there were simple switchback queues, like any airport security line. Later, Walt borrowed from Knott's Berry Farm the idea of hiding the queues. Still later, Disney's Imagineers—the corporate portmanteau to describe their "imagining" engineers—began making the line-standing experience not just an unfortunate side effect, but an integral part of the attraction.

Nowadays, what visitor to Disney World wouldn't feel a little remiss without at least walking through the queueing area? We might like the line to hurry along a little bit faster, perhaps, but to skip it entirely would be to miss a little bit of the magic.

In a system as large and complex as Disney World, all this is completely necessary. Designers need to focus on numbers, statistics, and processes, not the affirmation of each individual's inherent worth. Disney shows it cares by responding to the crowd, not the individual. Rides are designed with throughput always in mind. Disney engineers could design the most mind-blowing attraction in the world—time travel! space flights!—but if it could process only a couple of hundred people a day, what use would it be to them? They need to keep the crowds moving. You are a number to them, and be thankful for that. Your happiness depends upon it.

A Taxonomy of Theme Park Rides

Different kinds of rides present different challenges, depending on how they are loaded. For instance, you have stop-and-go loaders, such as Dumbo or the Mad Tea Party. These require the operator to completely stop the ride to let everyone disembark and embark each cycle. This creates a terribly low throughput. If they become backed up, there's not much Disney can do to speed things up, besides bringing in more employees to help load and unload or shortening the length of the ride (not a very satisfying solution for someone who has just waited an inordinate amount of time for that ride). Notably, these are older rides, already present in the 1950s (legacy rides, you might call them). It's doubtful that Disney would include them today, if they weren't so iconic.

I love Disney World, but I doubt many people would want to live on Main Street U.S.A. indefinitely. Disney World, like any pilgrimage, is meant to be a temporary experience. A few days. A week. At some point, you'll eventually want to go home, leaving the crowds, the control, the persistent surveillance behind you. I wouldn't be the first to note that there is something Orwellian about the entire operation, the way that individuals are strictly controlled and monitored.

More typical are interval loaders, such as roller coasters or the Pirates of the Caribbean ride. People can be loaded into and unloaded from cars while other cars are still moving through the ride. The ride never has to completely stop, greatly increasing efficiency and ensuring that system capacity isn't being wasted. Often an interval loader also has the virtue of being more flexible, adaptable to crowd conditions. Ride operators can simply add more cars when things are busy, and remove them when they are slow.

Finally, there are continuous loaders, rides that simply never stop moving, going on and on until someone flips the kill switch at the end of the day. Continuous loaders can also help relieve busy times by adding more cars to the conveyor belt.

Sure, there's nothing really sinister about it (it's not like anyone is putting a gun to your head to attend). But the kingdom is a kingdom, after all. An autocracy, however benign, is not a democracy (though arguably consumers vote by where they choose to spend their money). Let's agree to leave the benign Disney Surveillance State to Orlando, as a place not to live, but to visit.

Welcome to the least spontaneous place on earth.

Be Led Not by Whim

There's good news. Understanding how the park processes people is the first step to beating the crowds, if that's your desire. Crowds cluster because of spontaneity and whim. A thousand people at once individually decide that precisely now is the time to descend upon Space Mountain, creating a major logjam. Theoretically at least, you may share that whim with 47,000 others in the park at the same time. For their part, Disney does its best to mitigate the effects of whim. But the guest can do her part to avoid the lines as well, using the same kind of queueing theory information Disney uses. If long wait times at Space Mountain are more probable one hour and less probable another, you can act accordingly and avoid the wait.

Few of us are mathematicians. Fortunately, the work of studying Disney's queues mathematically has already been done, by Bob Sehlinger and Len Testa, the authors of *The Unofficial Guide to Walt Disney World* (which advertises its ability to "cut your waits in line by 4 hours a day"). If you're planning to visit the park and hate to stand in line, I can't recommend this book highly enough. It's a Bible—indeed, it's certainly Bible-size, getting ever bigger with each new edition—of theme park knowledge.

What's remarkable about the guide is the depth of research that went into it, by a small army of computer programmers, data analysts, and operations researchers who collected data, created models, and tested those models. They use this information to create an ideal touring plan—what order you should take the rides in, at what times—so as to spend the least amount of time possible in line. This is a daunting task when you consider that twenty-four different attractions means that there are "more than 620 billion trillion combinations" by which they can be visited.

Be led not by whim is the book's central message. "In many ways," Sehlinger writes, "Disney's theme parks are the quintessential system, the ultimate in mass-produced entertainment, the most planned and programmed environment. Lines for rides form in predictable ways at predictable times, for example, and you can either learn here how to avoid them or 'discover' them on your own."

One must become rigid and single-minded, following self-imposed rules and schedules. Sehlinger and his team create touring plans using the best available data. Do this, then that, then that other thing. Stick to the schedule. They preach that one must become as rigidly systematic as Disney is. Whim is your enemy. Gridlock happens because so many of us proceed without a plan and without data to guide us. In other words, to avoid standing in line, we have to somehow collectively agree to banish spontaneity from our lives, become fully machine-made at last. The way to skip the wait is numbers, data, statistics. So much for mystery. So much for magic. But at least your wait time will be reduced.

How to Avoid Standing in Line Completely

Sometimes when I'm sitting stuck in traffic, feeling frustrated, I like to think of the Borg, an alien race of cyborgs in the Star Trek universe, who operate at all times according to the "hive mind."

Half human and half machine, no one in the Borg Collective has a personality of its own; each member of the collective operates mechanically, unemotionally, a cog in the machine. The Borg are without a doubt the nastiest villain in the series, with the ability to assimilate enemies—and eventually the entire universe—into the hive. Their goal is to achieve perfection, through perfect coordination and streamlined efficiency, made possible only through the hive mind.

When I'm sitting in traffic, I think, *I bet the Borg wouldn't have put up with this!* They'd know how to perfectly coordinate traffic flow. The hive mind would dictate when each individual leaves the house. It would better utilize all hours of the day and night, dictating when each organism rests and works and for how long, based on the needs of the collective. There would never be gridlock, long lines, or any sort of glut whatsoever. They would instinctively employ the lessons of queueing theory. No wonder they're such a threat to the Star Trek universe.

But when I'm stuck in traffic? Suddenly, the Borg doesn't sound so bad.

Standing in line is reflective of mankind in a system, whether that system comprises school, work, cities, theme parks, traffic patterns, the military, health care, and so forth. Line standing is one way—the most iconic, but certainly not the only way—that we move through such systems.

Disney World is not unlike boot camp in this way. Only later would I note how strangely similar the two experiences were, like mirror images operating on the same general principle. Both are highly planned, "rational" environments. Both stress queue discipline. Both ask you to hurry up and wait, shuffle through one at a time, and keep to the schedule (only one, however, puts a premium on impeccably placed gift shops). Both are extreme manifestations of a certain form of social development, in this age of the crowd and the machine.

It feels like a paradox. As the example of the Borg illustrates, the more we are tamed to the conditions of queueing—the more we sacrifice our personal will to that of the system's—the less likely we would be to actually do so. In some science fiction future, we might develop the capability to agree with Borg-like unanimity to act according to efficiency, to perfectly coordinate our schedules with an eye to eliminating spontaneity and whim. Conversely, the fact that we still encounter lines in our lives—and the fact that we grumble about them, a very un-Borg-like reaction—shows that we remain human, all too human.

Still, it's never been easier to be a systems person. In some ways, most of us always were, based on experience and common sense, to the extent that we are able. Do your part. Don't drive during rush hour if you can avoid it. Avoid shopping after work or on weekends, and for god's sake, avoid Black Friday. The solution to beating the system is to become a systems person, always planning your day according to the probable behavior of others.

It is a small world. Nowadays, it lines up to be delivered to your doorstep. Thanks to technology, if you can work at home, one barely has to leave the house anymore. At this very moment, I can click a button on Amazon's website, and in two days UPS will deliver a package that has traveled across the country to get here.

I don't think most of us properly recognize the modern marvel that this is. And understanding the ways that queues form helped organize every step in that process, from the Internet that I use to the workings of that warehouse in Kentucky that my package ships from, the vast UPS hub it travels through, the hundreds of flights that must organized and ordered by air traffic controllers, and the truck that delivers it to your door. All this so that I don't have to put on pants and haul my ass to the store.

As someone who is crowd-shy, I find the option tempting. I have the ability to plan my day around the conscientious avoidance of others, with maximum efficiency in mind. The only surefire way to completely avoid standing in line is to never leave your house. A shut-in waits for no one. You can plan your day without worry that you're going to be at the back of the line somewhere, sighing and obsessively checking your watch. There are few surprises if you never risk venturing outdoors.

But perhaps some spontaneity of movement is both good and necessary. Perhaps there is value in risking the crowd and the wait. The pilgrimage is a tradition that goes back millennia in human history, an act of consciously joining hundreds and thousands of others at some sacred place, where there will doubtlessly be long lines to the bathroom, the concession stand, to reserve a table at a restaurant.

Has the act of waiting itself ever been considered sacred, with a religious function of its own? (Or how about the line to see St. Peter at the Pearly Gates? Is that first come, first served?) I don't know. But I'm willing to bet there's something that drives people to theme parks that exceeds the value of the relatively short moments of fun they have on the rides. And I suspect that people who line up outside stores the night before Black Friday are doing so for reasons that exceed the value of the discount they'll receive on a new flat-screen TV.

I'm not saying I would ever go out of my way to stand in line. Should we be sad that modern science and technology are streamlining—rationalizing, systemizing, making more efficient—the ways we wait? Of course not. There's nothing fun about waiting, and short of cutting in line, I don't begrudge anyone's attempts to avoid the queue. But maybe to completely banish spontaneity and the risk of waiting from our lives means giving up something important to the human experience.

If we planned our day solely according to efficiency, I think we'd miss out on a lot of things: good conversations, a good book, that profound thought that sneaks up on you while you're waiting to see the dentist. We'd also miss the indelible experience of bitching about the wait with our fellow line standers.

So by all means, I encourage people to leave the house, make the pilgrimage. Go about your day without discipline, without a plan. Don't be like the Borg. Leave maximizing system efficiency to the likes of Disney. Stay untamed. You might find yourself waiting in line, sure. That's always the risk, but I'm pretty sure it's worth it. It's part of what makes us human.

Meanwhile, when you're at a crowded supermarket, which line should you choose to stand in? Does it matter? How much does a few minutes cost you? Besides, the other line will always move faster anyway. As we know from the psychology of queueing, half the problem is perception. Our minds are rigged against us. Regardless of time actually spent, the slowest line will always be the one you personally are standing in. So relax. Distract yourself. Stay zen. Be alone with your thoughts. Be kind to your cashier. Because standing in line is a state of mind.

ABOUT THE AUTHOR

David Andrews was raised in Bucharest, Romania, and Yacolt, Washington, and did a stint in the U.S. Navy as a Russian linguist.